Estorick Collection of modern italian art

The Enchanted Room
Modern Works from the Pinacoteca di Brera

Published on the occasion of the exhibition

The Enchanted Room
Modern Works from the Pinacoteca di Brera

24 January – 8 April 2018

Exhibition organised by: Estorick Collection of Modern Italian Art
Roberta Cremoncini; Christopher Adams

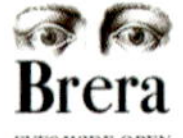 Pinacoteca di Brera
James M. Bradburne; Marina Gargiulo; Elisabetta Bianchi;
Alessandro Coscia; Emanuela Daffra; Alessandra Quarto

This exhibition has been made possible as a result of the Government Indemnity
Scheme. The Estorick Collection would like to thank HM Government for providing
indemnity and the Department for Digital, Culture, Media and Sport and Arts Council
England for arranging the indemnity.

Catalogue translations by: Christopher Adams

Catalogue designed by: Gordon Mills (Gordon Mills Design Ltd)

Public Relations: Alison Wright PR

External Relations Advisor: Enrica de Biasi

Technical Sponsors:

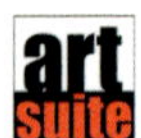 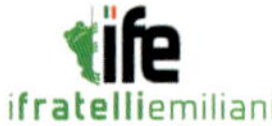 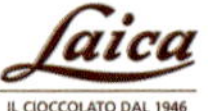 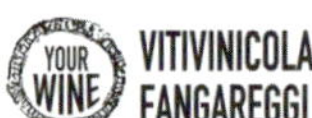

Cover image:
Carlo Carrà
The Metaphysical Muse, 1917
Oil on canvas, 90 x 66 cm

Contents

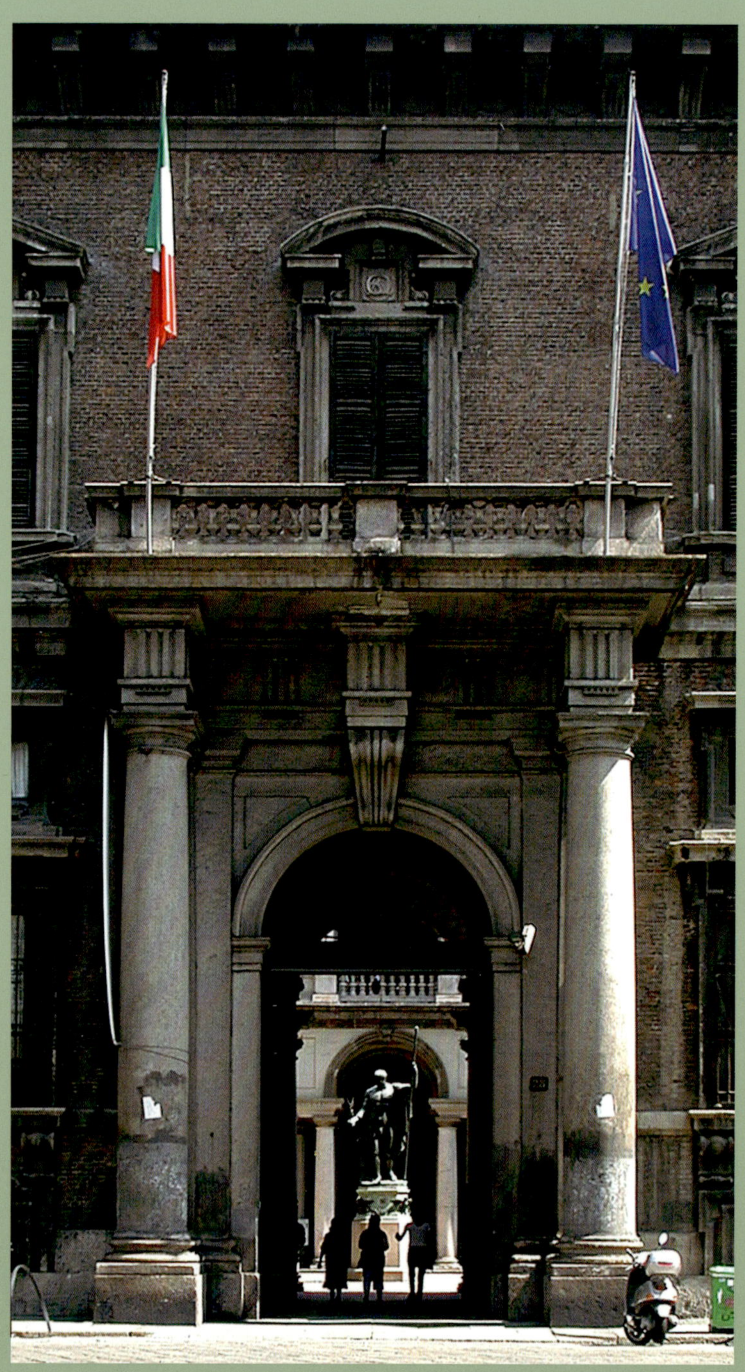

Introduction

January 2018 marks the twentieth anniversary of the opening of the Estorick Collection at its home in Islington, and *The Enchanted Room* is a fitting exhibition with which to celebrate this important landmark. The title of the show – taken from a painting of the same name by Carlo Carrà – was chosen not only because it conveys the idea of something magical, but also something small and private. The works on display represent the choices of two collectors who had a deep and special relationship with each of their paintings, while our own museum has an intimate atmosphere that enables our visitors to connect with art in a particularly personal manner.

During the last two decades we have explored collections similar to ours by way of comparing and contrasting different approaches and tastes. Previous exhibitions have presented the collection of Paola and Marta Giovanardi (1999), and that of Alberto Della Ragione (2011). Like Eric and Salome Estorick, Emilio and Maria Jesi were passionate about Italian art and their collection has many points of contact with our own. They were collecting at the same time, and shared an interest in many of the same artists – and sometimes, the same artworks (both collections contain studies for Umberto Boccioni's masterpiece *The City Rises*, for instance). However, the Estoricks were more interested in the work of art itself – the quality of each one being of paramount importance – rather than the artists. This was partly because the Estoricks did not live in Italy and did not speak the language. In contrast, the Jesi established relationships not only with artists but also with galleries and the whole art world, highlighting a completely different way of relating to works of art.

We are very privileged to be showing an important part of the Jesi Collection outside Italy for the first time, and to collaborate with the world famous Pinacoteca di Brera which houses it. The desire of its Director, James Bradburne, to raise the profile of the Pinacoteca's modern collection fits perfectly with our own ambition of showcasing the best of modern Italian art, and of introducing its collectors to the British public.

I would like to thank James for his enthusiasm and guidance during the preparations for this exhibition, as well as Marina Gargiulo, Curator of the Modern Collections, and her colleagues at the Pinacoteca: Emanuela Daffra, Alessandra Quarto and Elisabetta Bianchi. My gratitude goes to my colleagues at the Estorick Collection – Christopher Adams, Luke Alder and Claudia Zanardi, whose hard work and enthusiasm enables the Estorick Collection to achieve such splendid results – and Sue Bond and Maria de Peverelli, Trustees of the Estorick Foundation, for their introduction to James, and for their relentless support. Lastly, my thanks go to Enrica de Biasi and the sponsors of our opening night.

Roberta Cremoncini
Director

The Jesi Collection at the Estorick – A Showcase on Collecting

Milan has never been a city of memories, and has always wanted to be able to respond fully to the needs and character of its own time, to be contemporary in each historical moment, with an open civic and poetic spirit[1]

Franco Russoli, 1956

The story of art is also the story of collectors, collections and museums. This exhibition of the Jesi Collection at the Estorick allows the public to deepen its understanding of the relationship between artists, collectors and the museums that often end up as hosts to the collectors' legacy. It shines a light on four collectors, Emilio Jesi and his wife Maria, and on Eric Estorick and his wife Salome. It also reveals the importance of two institutions and their directors, the Estoricks in London, who decided to reject offers to sell their collection and instead created their own museum, and the Pinacoteca di Brera in Milan, whose visionary Director Franco Russoli (1923–1977) brought to Brera the collections of the city's greatest post-war collectors.

On 21 March 1977, a few days before Bruno Munari's innovative educational laboratory was to open at the Pinacoteca di Brera, Franco Russoli died of a heart attack at only 54 years old. With him died a vision of Brera as a place of civility and citizenship, and of the museum as the place where we rediscover the wellsprings of our identity as members of contemporary society.

Brera already had a long history by 1977. Originally founded as a convent in the fourteenth century, the palace was designed in 1615 for the College of the Jesuit Order and finally completed by Piermarini in 1776. Under the Jesuits, a Catholic order with a deep interest in the new sciences, Brera was home to a botanical garden and the city's first observatory. Brera was taken in hand by the Empress Maria Teresa in 1773, who enhanced the botanical garden and founded the Academy for the Fine Arts and the Braidense Library. In 1808 Napoleon, recognising the diversity of its institutions, baptised it the Royal Palace of the Arts and Sciences. Extensively bombed in 1943, with only one exhibition space left covered, Brera was repaired under the watchful eye of Fernanda Wittgens after the war, and fully restored by 1950.

Russoli belonged to the generation that helped rebuild Europe after World War II, in which he was part of the Resistance, as was his near contemporary Willem Sandberg, later Director of Amsterdam's Stedelijk Museum. It was a generation who came fully of age in the '60s and '70s, fired by a vision in which the museum was a fundamental weapon in the struggle

"

against the forces that had dragged Europe through two world wars and left its cultural capitals and cultural capital in ruins. Russoli, Sandberg, Goodman and many others saw the museum's mission as the "making and re-making" of the world they lived in[2] – a return to the Enlightenment values which had seen the birth of the world's first truly public museums in France at the end of the eighteenth century.

Franco Russoli believed a museum should stay contemporary, and as a specialist in modern art himself, cultivated a circle of the most important post-war Milanese collectors of Italian art: Gianni Mattioli, Lamberto Vitali, Emilio Jesi and Riccardo Jucker. By the time of his death in 1977, all four of their collections had been committed to Brera. Unfortunately, with Russoli's death, and the creation of the new Ministry of Culture, the museum's priorities changed. The Jucker Collection was sold to the city, where it became the core of the Museum of 20th Century Art that opened in 2010. Gianni Mattioli's collection, which Russoli had intended for the Brera, was left to his daughter. The Palazzo Citterio, purchased in 1972 to house the Brera's modern collections, suffered setback after setback, and had to wait until 2013 when funds were finally found to finish refitting it. Finally, in 2019, the Palazzo Citterio will open to the public as Brera Modern – The Museum of Italian Modern and Contemporary Art. At its core will be the Jesi, Mattioli and Vitali Collections, enhanced by a selection of key loans from Milanese and international museums.

The exhibition of the Jesi Collection at the Estorick is therefore of enormous historical significance. On the one hand it is the first time a major part of the collection has been shown outside of Italy, where it will be seen at the museum of two of England's foremost collectors of modern Italian art. On the other, it is a preview of the permanent collection that will open at Brera Modern in less than a year's time. Franco Russoli believed in collecting, collectors and collections, and believed that they were an essential part of the museum's mission to remain at the heart of contemporary society. This exhibition provides an exceptional opportunity for the public take a glimpse inside the minds of four great collectors of modern Italian art, Emilio and Maria Jesi and Eric and Salome Estorick.

It has been a pleasure and a privilege to make it possible for the Jesi Collection to be seen at the Estorick. I would like to thank the Estorick's Board, especially Maria de Peverelli and Sue Bond, who strongly supported the idea of this exhibition from the outset. I would like to thank the Estorick's Director, Roberta Cremoncini, for her tenacity and persistence. I would like to thank the exhibition's curators and all those who have worked on the show: at the Estorick, Christopher Adams, Claudia Zanardi and Luke Alder; at the Pinacoteca, Marina Gargiulo, ably supported by Elisabetta Bianchi and Alessandro Coscia, as well as the curatorial staff under the leadership of Emanuela Daffra, and the operations staff under the direction of Alessandra Quarto. Without all of them, this exhibition would never have seen the light of day.

James M. Bradburne
General Director, Pinacoteca di Brera e Biblioteca Nazionale Braidense

---

[1] "Milano non è mai stata una città di ricordi, e in ogni epoca ha voluto essere in grado di rispondere pienamente alle esigenze e al carattere del tempo, essere sempre contemporanea di ogni momento storico, con aperto spirito civile e poetico."

[2] "The museum has to function as an institution for the prevention of blindness in order to make works work [...] Works work when, by stimulating inquisitive looking, sharpening perception, raising visual intelligence, they participate in [...] the making and re-making of our worlds"; Nelson Goodman, 1980.

This collection of the art of our time
entrusted to the State
is dedicated to the artists and art lovers
of yesterday, today and tomorrow

Emilio and Maria Jesi

The Jesi Collection at the Pinacoteca di Brera

The history of the formation of the Pinacoteca di Brera's collections is bound up with the birth of the Accademia di Belle Arti – that is, to a gallery of paintings, sculptures and etchings intended to be used for educational purposes – and to the collection of ecclesiastical works assembled as a consequence of the suppression of the convents by Napoleon Bonaparte, crowned King of Italy in 1805. It was therefore a museum created by the will of the state, rather than one formed of works collected by the nobility, in contrast to the Uffizi, Capodimonte or Borghese galleries. During the twentieth century, this extraordinary patrimony was built on by a number of donations and important bequests reflecting modern collecting practices. Thanks to the commitment of Franco Russoli (1923-1977), who became Director of Brera in 1973, the museum which had long been renowned for its historical collections began to give room to the work of great artists (many of whom were still alive) represented in the most important private Milanese collections of contemporary art. In fact, many collectors – including the Jesi – found in Russoli a sympathetic figure, open to dialogue and collaboration. The 1970s were a time of great change and renewal for the museum. In December 1974, Riccardo Jucker donated a collection of 18 Futurist paintings to the Pinacoteca that were intended for permanent exhibition; unfortunately, these were withdrawn by Jucker's heirs in 1990 and subsequently given to the City of Milan, which currently exhibits them at the Museo del' 900. Also during Russoli's tenure, 15 of the museum's rooms – including the Braidense Library – were given over to the exhibition *Processo per il museo*, which presented works by a number of contemporary artists freely inspired by Brera's ancient collections, including both Italian and foreign figures such as Henry Moore, Graham Sutherland, Renato Guttuso, Fausto Melotti, Giacomo Manzù, Bruno Munari, Giulio Paolini and Enrico Baj.

Emilio and Maria Jesi's collection of paintings and sculptures represented the most innovative approach to collecting during the 1930s and '40s, bringing together representative examples of works by renowned artists affiliated with the most important modern art movements (Futurism, Metaphysical art, Novecento) such as Umberto Boccioni, Giorgio Morandi, Carlo Carrà, Amedeo Modigliani, Mario Sironi, Filippo de Pisis and Marino Marini, to name but a few. True lovers of the art of their time, Emilio Jesi (a businessman and entrepreneur) and his wife Maria did not limit themselves simply to acquiring pieces that satisfied their individual tastes, but personally associated with painters and sculptors, often receiving them in their apartment at Palazzo Citterio, located near the Pinacoteca di Brera, the rooms of which were entirely covered by their precious collection. Gian Alberto Dell'Acqua – who worked at, and was Director of Brera from 1935 to 1973 – recalls "the particular and unique atmosphere created by the reciprocal relationship between certain works in certain domestic environments. [...] the rigorous arrangement of paintings by Carrà and de Chirico in the living room, the Morandi room, the glittering collection of works by de Pisis covering the walls of the bedroom. The long-awaited arrival of a new painting [...] was enough to provoke a small revolution in the sagacious ordering of the collection. Having judiciously placed the most recent purchase, the owner was then happy to present it proudly to his visitors."[1]

Fortunately, the farsighted cultural project of the Jesi was not limited to the formation of a sort of 'manual' of twentieth-century Italian art history, but had as its natural conclusion the generous decision to present that patrimony of masterpieces to a wider public, selecting the Pinacoteca di Brera for its home – especially, a new section of the museum, originally intended to be located in Palazzo Citterio.

The building was bought by the state in 1972 with the aim of renewing and modernising the Pinacoteca, and substantially contributing to Russoli's ambitious project for a new, modern *Grande Brera*: an enlarged Brera, offering educational services, archives, workshops, conference rooms and exhibition halls both for temporary exhibitions and for works from the permanent collection, comprising donations of important private collections of modern art.

Convinced of the eternal intrinsic and educational value of art, and in agreement with the ideas of Russoli on the need to make the museum as up-to-date as possible, the Jesi allocated 80 works to the state, intending them to be displayed at Palazzo Citterio with the phrase: This collection of the art of our time / entrusted to the State / is dedicated to the artists and art lovers / of yesterday, today and tomorrow / Emilio and Maria Jesi. The actual transfer of the works, which took place between 1975 and 1976 following the death of Emilio, was overseen by Maria. The initial donation comprised 50 paintings and 5 sculptures, while the remaining works were given to Brera in 1984.[2] In 1982, Russoli's successor Carlo Bertelli exhibited part of the donation to the public for the first time – together with the Jucker Collection – in a new wing of the museum, the so-called Astronomer's Apartment, renovated by Ignazio Gardella. Only since 2003 has it been possible to admire the collection in its entirety, in the long and narrow Sala X (flanked, in Sala XI, by another key collection of twentieth-century art

donated by America and Lamberto Vitali). The works are displayed with an innovative and unusual hanging system specially designed for paintings of modest dimensions, with alarmed metal supports and panels arranged obliquely in relation to the walls in order to increase the available display surfaces, and equipped with bases and showcases for the sculptures of Marino Marini, Arturo Martini and Medardo Rosso. Marini's bronze portrait of Emilio Jesi (1947)[3] appears alongside the donors' dedicatory statement.

Works by one of the key artists represented in the Jesi Collection had already been hosted in the halls of the Pinacoteca many years prior to their definitive arrival. In 1942, Carlo Carrà mounted a solo show curated by Guglielmo Pacchioni and Gian Alberto Dell'Acqua, in collaboration with the Centro di Azioni per le Arti (Centre of Action for the Arts), comprising 114 paintings and numerous etchings and drawings. The show included a number of paintings dating from 1917 included in the present exhibition, then identified as the property of a certain 'Della Lanterna', a name chosen by Emilio Jesi for reasons of confidentiality.[4] It is probable that this first concrete interaction with the museum by the collector, who "closely followed and warmly supported" the initiative,[5] laid the foundations for his subsequent donation. Created during Carrà's enforced period of recuperation at the military hospital in Villa del Seminario near Ferrara,[6] *Mother and Son*, *The Metaphysical Muse* and *The Enchanted Room* illustrate the artist's highly personal adhesion to the Metaphysical iconography of de Chirico. By this point, Carrà had left behind his Cubo-Futurist phase, represented by the intersecting planes and lyrical chromatic harmonies of *Rhythms of Objects* (1911). The two distinct phases of Carrà's work also seem to have corresponded to the aesthetic predilections of the Jesi themselves. In terms of the Metaphysical tendency, this led to their purchasing extraordinary examples of Morandi's work, such as the various still lifes and rural landscapes depicting the artist's beloved village of Grizzana. Also in this vein is the art of Mario Sironi, as illustrated by the solid and impressive volume of *The Truck* (1914-15) and *The Lamp* (1919) – the final version of which appears to have been heavily modified with respect to the initial composition, visible by means of scientific imaging techniques – as well as in his adherence to the aesthetics of the Novecento school, which led him to express the desolation of the contemporary industrial and urban world in pure and lyrical forms (*Urban Landscape with Truck*, 1919-20; *Urban Landscape with Chimney*, 1930).

The collectors' interest in the Cubo-Futurist aesthetic is witnessed by the presence of markedly geometric works by Gino Severini (*Large Still Life with Pumpkin*, 1917; *Le Nord-Sud*, 1912), Ottone Rosai (*Still Life: The Carpenter's Bench*, 1914) and Ardengo Soffici (*Watermelon and Liqueurs*, 1914), the latter artist also being represented by a work in a more naturalistic style, redolent of the French avant-gardes (*Santa Cristina*, 1908).

The works of Filippo de Pisis – who is represented in the Collection by more pieces than any other artist – reveal his ability to assimilate and rework, in accordance with his personal sensibility, not only the most advanced trends of the time (Metaphysical imagery in *Sacred Fish*, 1925 and *Marine Still Life with Shrimps*, 1926) but also of the recent past, as illustrated by the Impressionist overtones of *San Moisè* (1930).

Although few portraits were collected by the Jesi, two beautiful works by Amedeo Modigliani dedicated to his friend the painter Moïse Kisling and a female figure (*Head of a Young Woman*, 1915) testify to the singular and iconic approach to the genre adopted by this master.

Symbolising the museum's decision to engage with more recent art in 1949 is the large *Self Portrait* by Umberto Boccioni (1908): a work that was donated by Vico Baer, and now perfectly integrated with the Jesi Collection. Boccioni painted this work on the back of another self portrait that he subsequently abandoned. Having recently undergone restoration, which has made the details more intelligible, this image depicts a truly *plein air* scene, with the artist in the foreground, palette in hand, against an urban backdrop of buildings, a railway, a canal and industrial buildings shown from an elevated viewpoint. The panorama was probably taken from a terrace or a balcony of the room where the artist lived in 1907 in the Milanese suburbs of the early twentieth century, with the Acquabella viaduct and numerous houses under construction captured as if in a snapshot. It is the picture that marked the Brera's transition to the modern era, yet Boccioni was not at all satisfied with it, writing in a letter: "I have finished a self portrait that leaves me completely indifferent. I'm tired and I have no ideas."

Marina Gargiulo
Head of Collections
Pinacoteca di Brera

---

[1] G. A. Dall'Acqua, *La donazione Emilio e Maria Jesi* (Quaderni di Brera), Milan, 1981, p. 9. On the Jesi donation, see also: M. Cresseri, 'Emilio Jesi – Maria Arrighi', in *Per Brera. Collezionisti e doni alla Pinacoteca dal 1882 al 2000*, ed. by M. Ceriana, C. Quattrini and M. Cresseri (Quaderni di Brera, 10), Florence, Centro Di, 2000, pp. 201-03; D. Pescarmona, 'L'irrompere della modernità dell'Ottocento e del Novecento nella Pinacoteca di Brera. Un momento di svolta nella problematica continuità del museo napoleonico (Fernanda Wittgens e Franco Russoli)', in *Storie scritte a Brera (2014-1776)*, Sondrio, 2017, pp. 22, 30-31, 33-34.

[2] For a detailed chronology of the donation, see Pescarmona, 'L'irrompere…', cit., p. 31.

[3] S. Fontana, 'Scheda n. 857', in *Pinacoteca di Brera. Dipinti dell'Ottocento e del Novecento*, II; Milan, 1994, pp. 761-62.

[4] *Carlo Carrà 1881-1966*, exh. cat., ed. by A. Monferini (Rome, Galleria Nazionale d'Arte Moderna, 15 December 1994 – 28 February, 1995), Milan, Electa, 1994, pp. 11-14, 35-37.

[5] Dall'Acqua, *La donazione…*, cit., p. 15.

[6] Assigned to the 27th Infantry Regiment of Ferrara, as a simple soldier, in January 1917 Carlo Carrà was declared unfit and entrusted to the psychiatric care of the neurological section of Villa del Seminario, a hospital located a few kilometers from Ferrara, where Giorgio de Chirico, Alberto Savinio and Mario Pozzati were also hospitalised with a diagnosis of neurasthenia. See *De Chirico a Ferrara. Metafisica e avanguardia*, exh. cat., ed. by P. Baldacci, G. Ross (Ferrara, Palazzo dei Diamanti, 14 November 2015 - 28 February 2016), Ferrara, 2015, pp. 97-101.

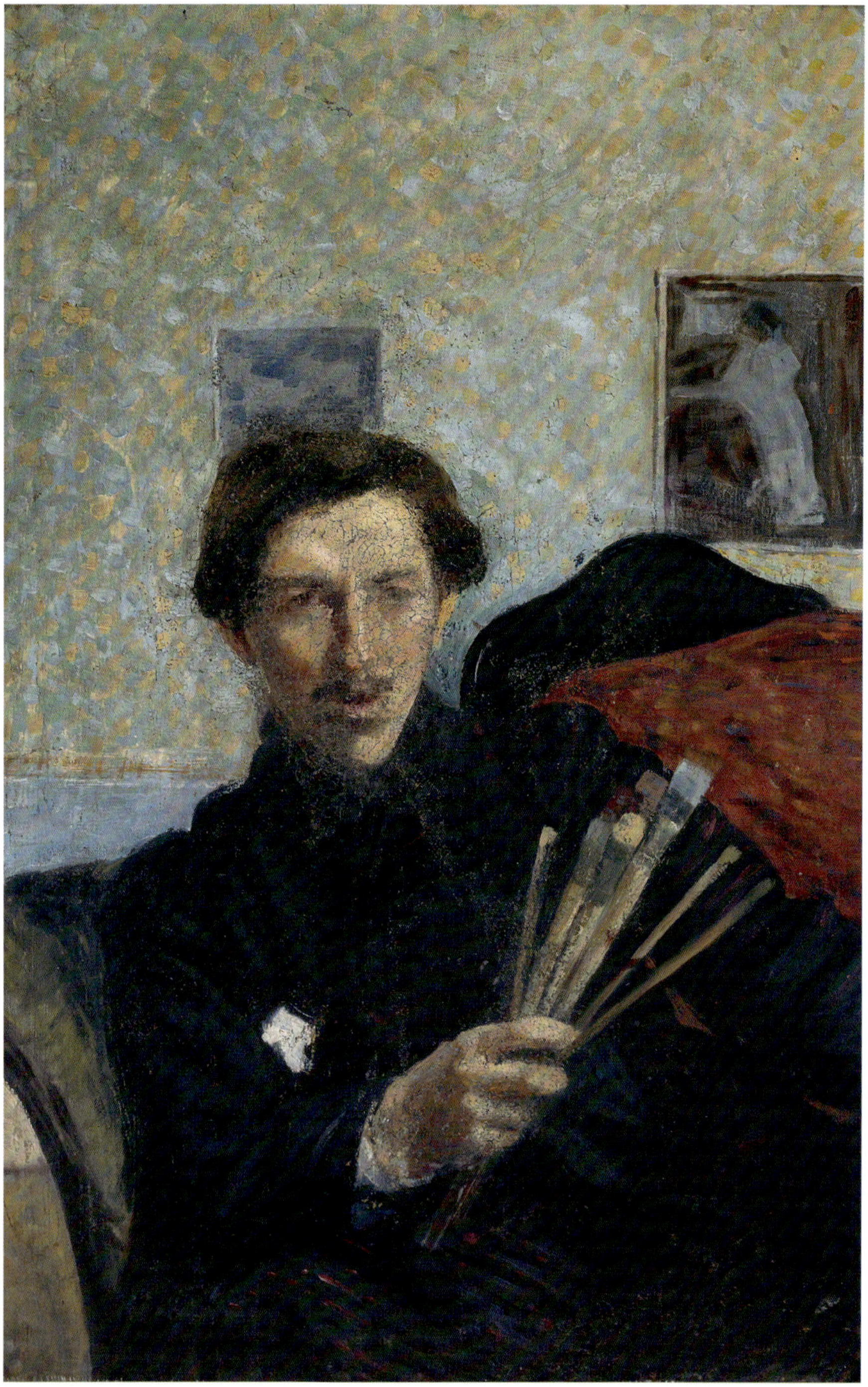

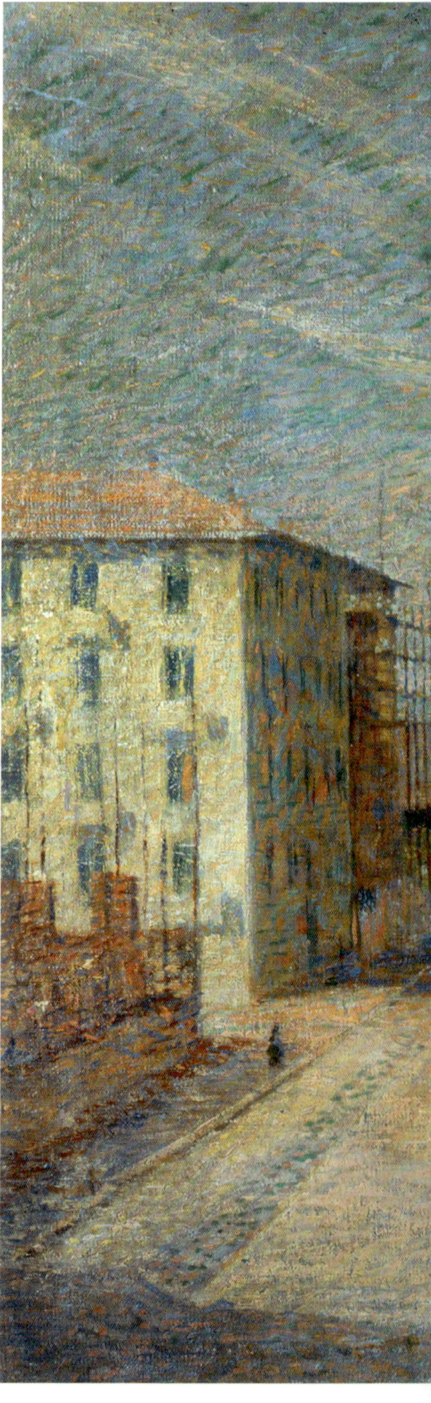

Umberto Boccioni
Self Portrait (verso), c. 1906-07
Oil on canvas, 100 x 70 cm

Umberto Boccioni
Self Portrait (recto), 1908
Oil on canvas, 70 x 100 cm

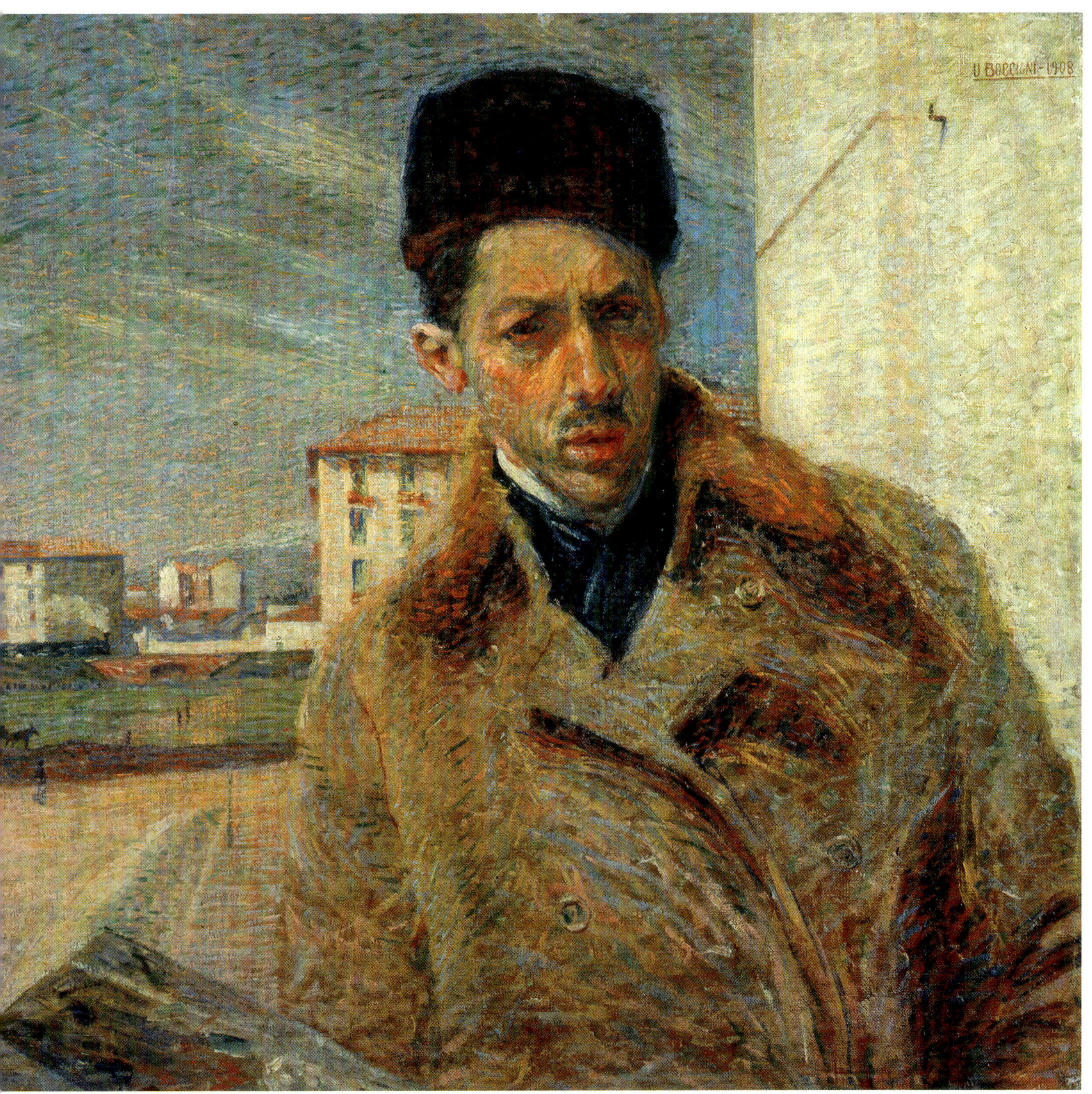

This *Self Portrait* was painted by Boccioni in his studio on Via Adige, Milan. Rendered in the broken brushstrokes of the Divisionist style, the urban background hints at his subsequent Futurist interests, featuring in later works such as *The City Rises*. The portrait was donated to Brera by Boccioni's friend and collector, Vico Baer.

On the back of the painting is another self portrait, which would seem to be an earlier work judging by its style and the sitter's youthful features. This second image was almost completely hidden beneath a layer of grey paint, and reveals a certain hesitation in its composition; it was probably painted over by Boccioni himself because he was dissatisfied with the result.

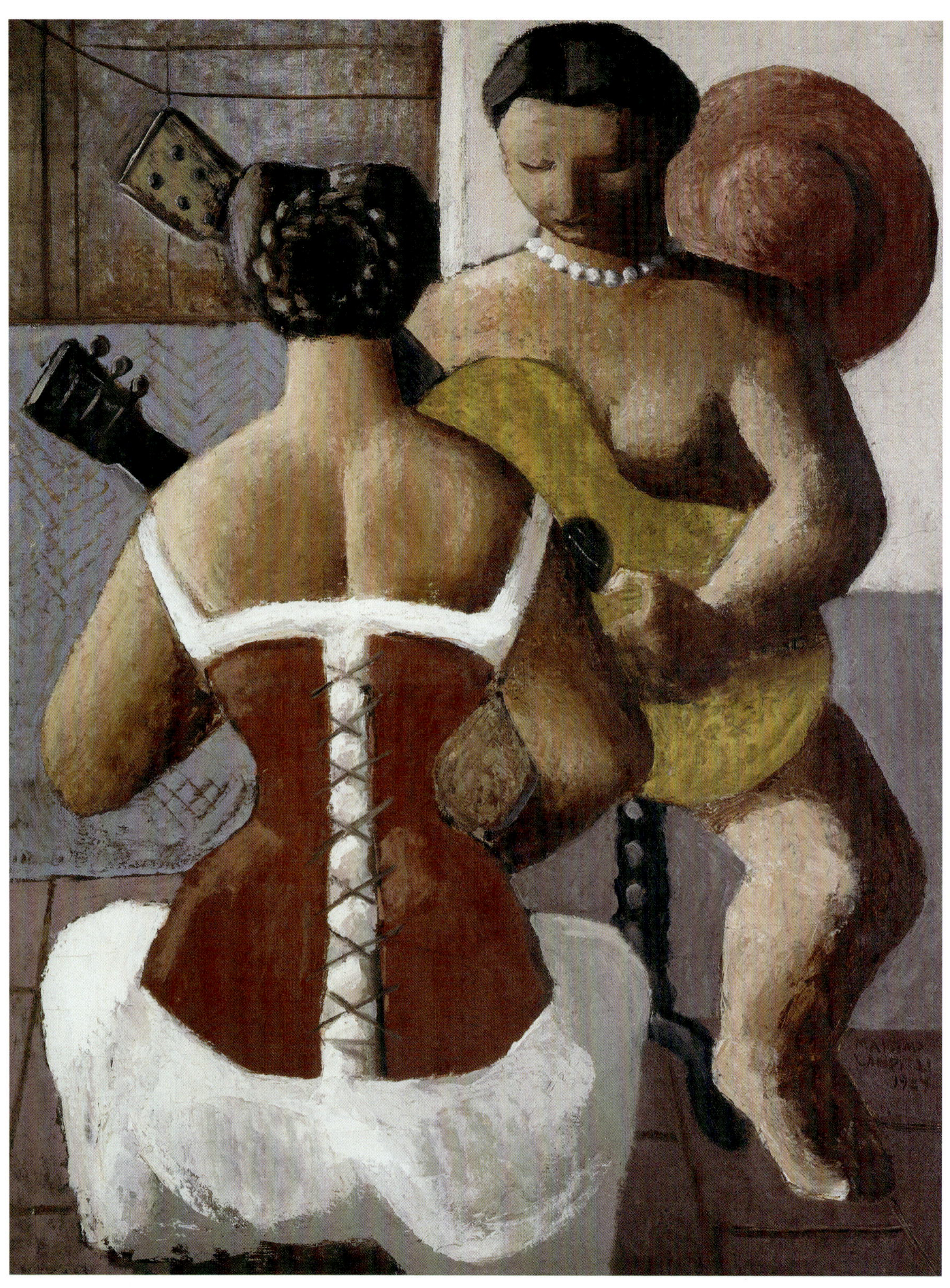

Massimo Campigli
Women with Guitar, 1927
Oil on canvas, 93.4 x 72.2 cm

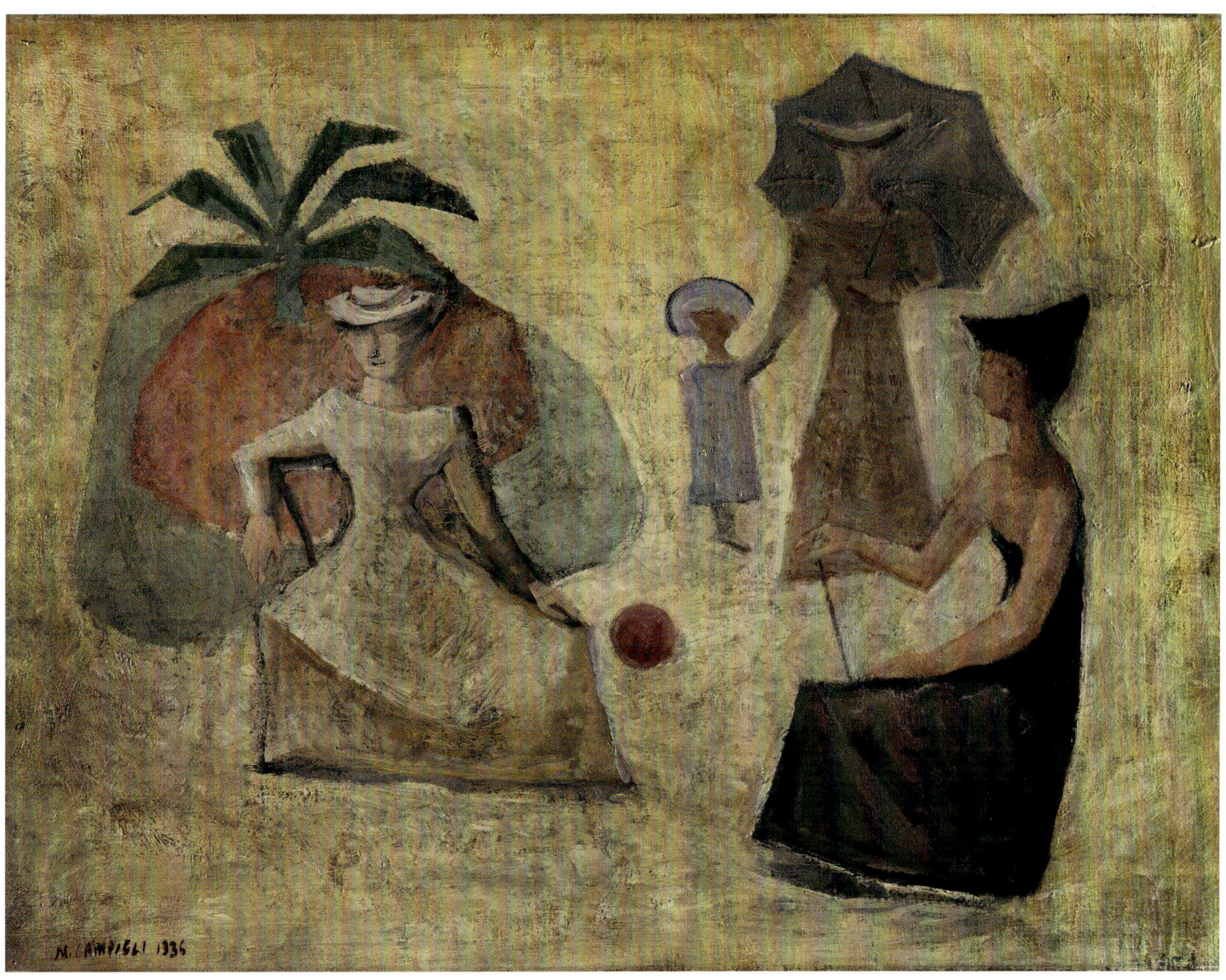

Massimo Campigli
The Garden, 1936
Oil on canvas, 73 x 92 cm

Women with Guitar was purchased for the Pinacoteca in 1995, and is a good example of Campigli's work between 1924 and 1927. Campigli moved to Paris in 1919, where he worked as a correspondent for the *Corriere della Sera* and became familiar with the vocabularies of Picasso and Léger, as well as the 'primitive' imagery explored by the capital's avant-garde circles. Inspired by such influences, this canvas depicts simplified figures informed by post-Cubist aesthetics and treated with those opaque, earthy colours typical of the austere and rigorous approach formulated by Campigli at this time.

Returning to Milan in 1931, Campigli continued to develop the formal stylisation he had first explored during the previous decade. *The Garden* is emblematic of the artist's Milanese period, being permeated by a magical, dreamlike atmosphere, and inhabited by figures transformed into pure geometric forms in which the influence of Picasso is enriched with suggestions from 'primitive' and Etruscan art.

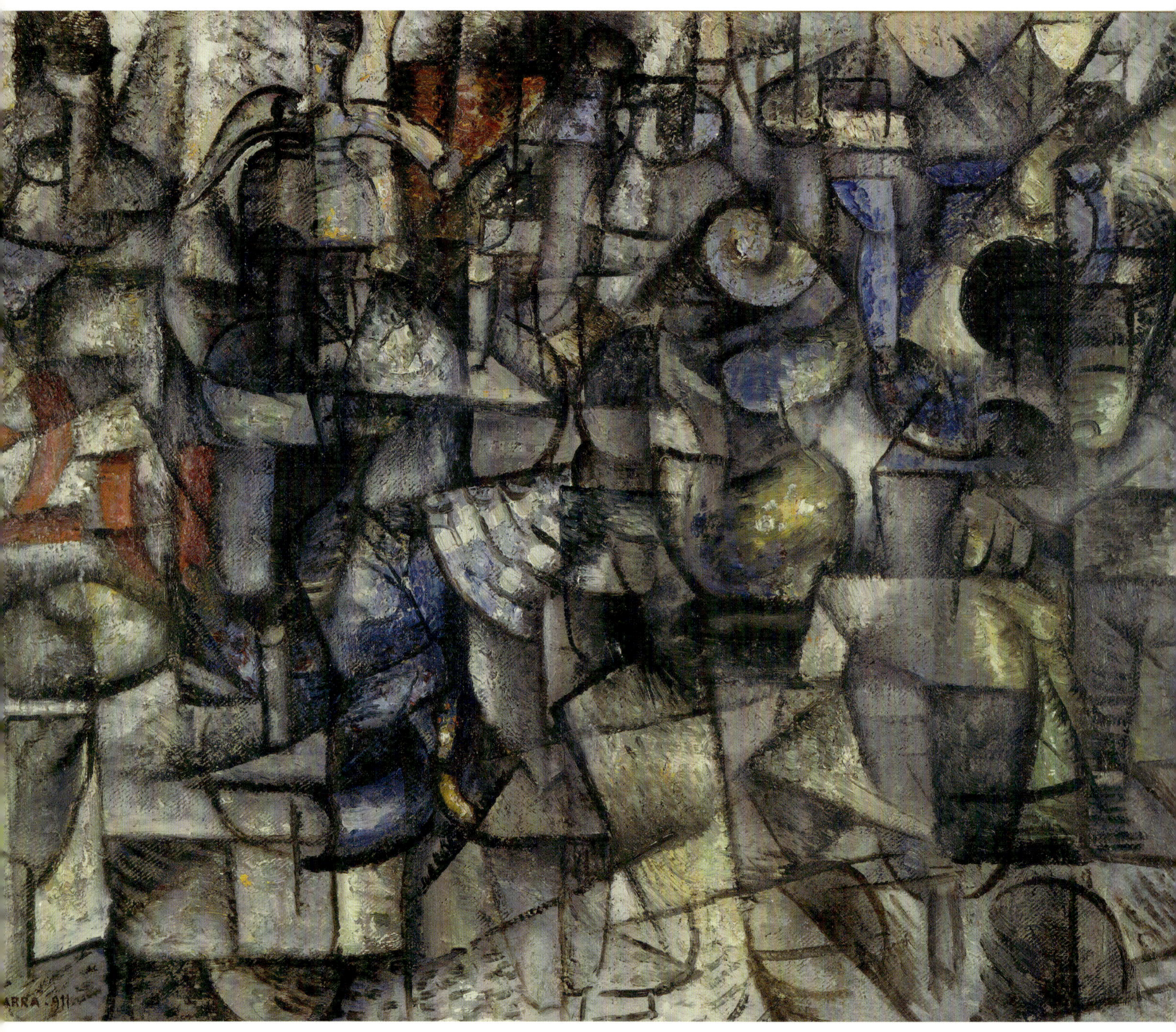

Carlo Carrà
Rhythms of Objects, 1911
Oil on canvas, 53 x 67 cm

The works on display in the present exhibition provide an overview of Carrà's stylistic development during the first two decades of the twentieth century. In 1908, he began to associate with the group of artists who would go on to pioneer Futurist painting, and in 1911 he visited Paris with Umberto Boccioni, where he was introduced to Cubism by his colleague Gino Severini. Both influences fed directly into *Rhythms of Objects*, in which the formal austerity of the Cubist aesthetic is combined with Futurist themes of movement, simultaneity and the interpenetration of planes.

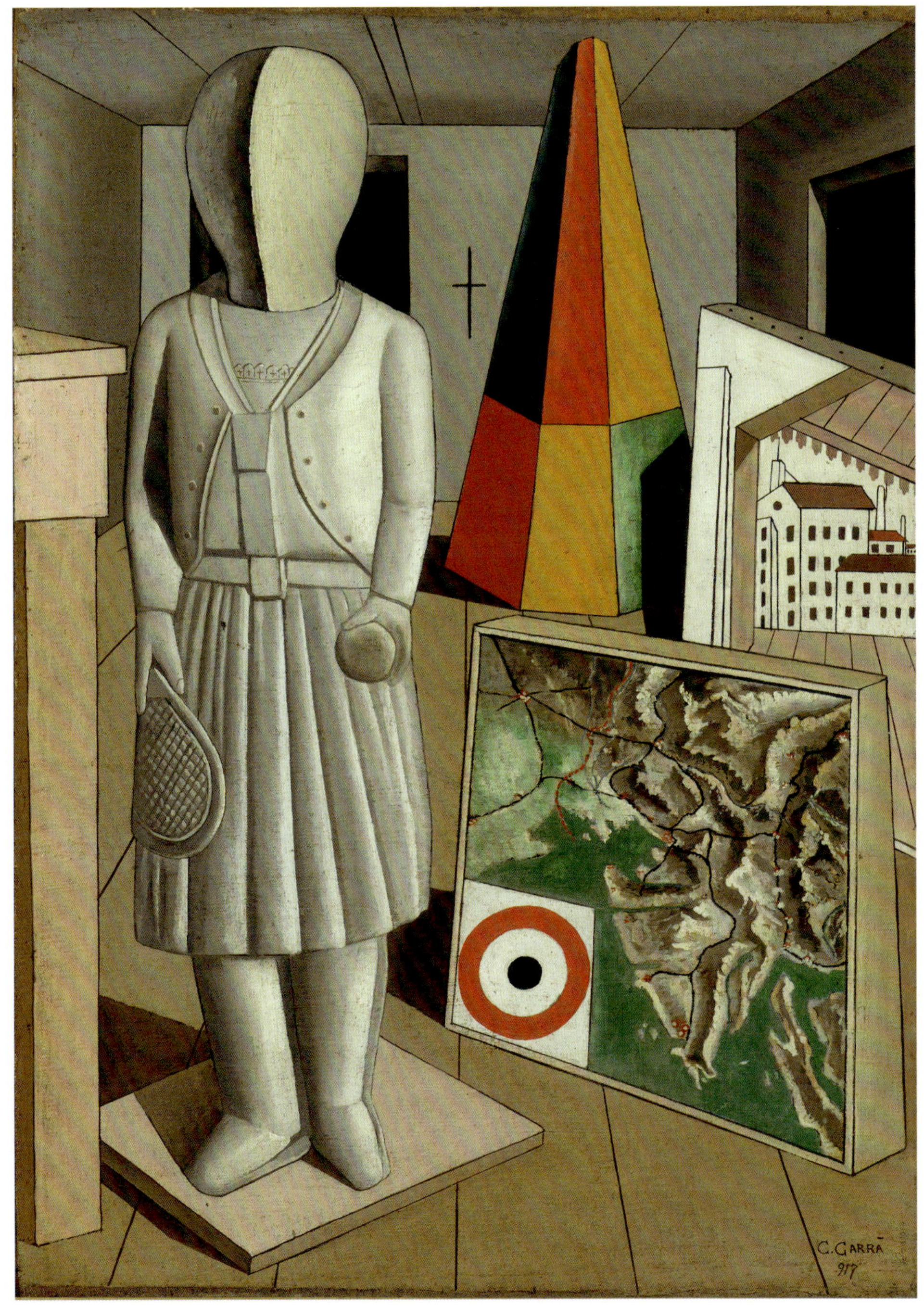

Carlo Carrà
The Metaphysical Muse, 1917
Oil on canvas, 90 x 66 cm

In 1917, Carrà met Giorgio de Chirico and Filippo de Pisis and adopted the
language of Metaphysical art, a phase represented here by three paintings of
that year (*The Metaphysical Muse, The Enchanted Room* and *Mother and Son*).
In these works, the artist reinterpreted the iconography favoured by de Chirico as
a means of exploring the pure forms of 'ordinary things'. He stayed true to these
concerns over the following years, progressively withdrawing from the excesses of
the avant-garde and promoting a return to the classical origins of Italian figurative
art, typified by painters such as Giotto.

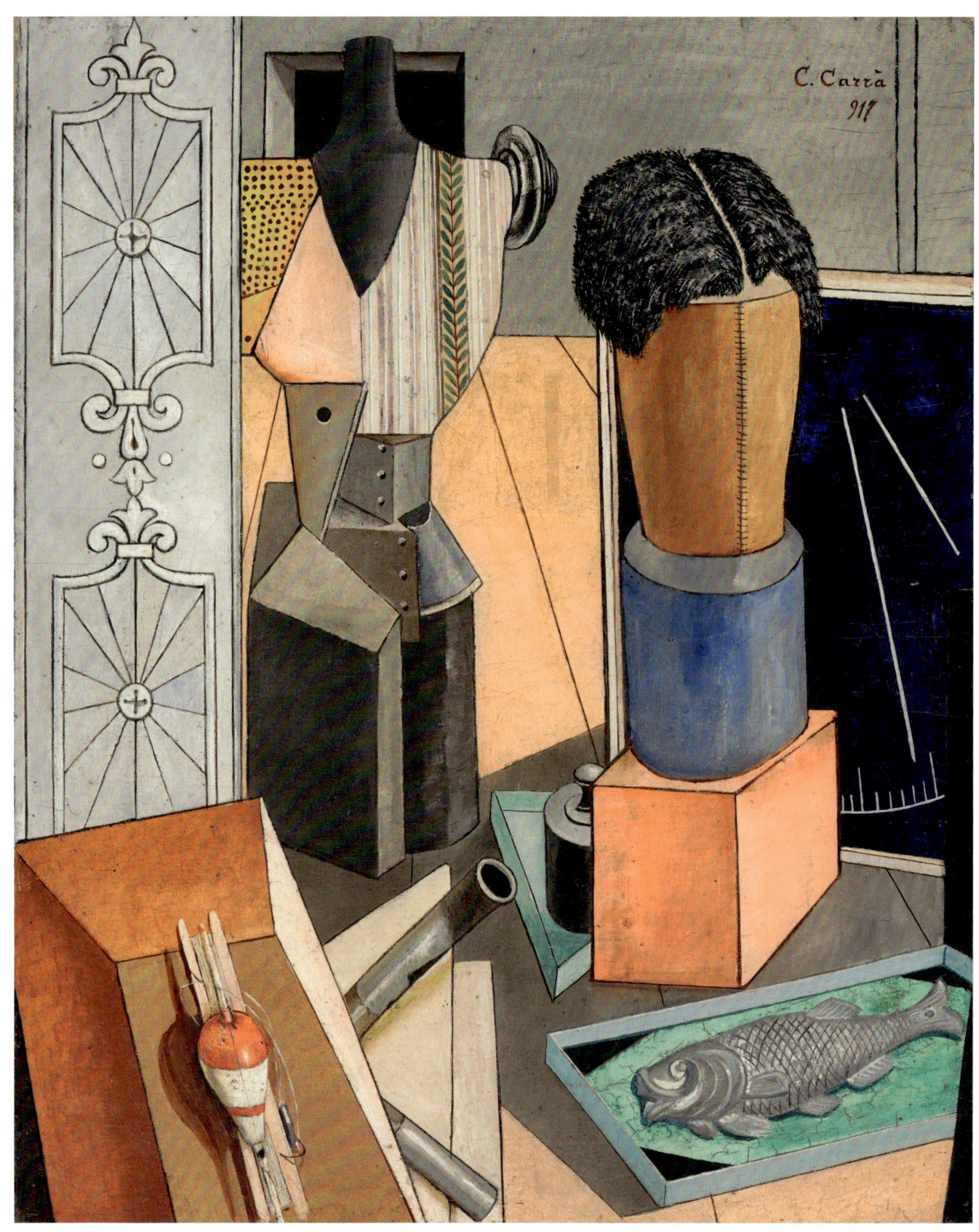

Carlo Carrà
The Enchanted Room, 1917
Oil on canvas, 68 x 52 cm

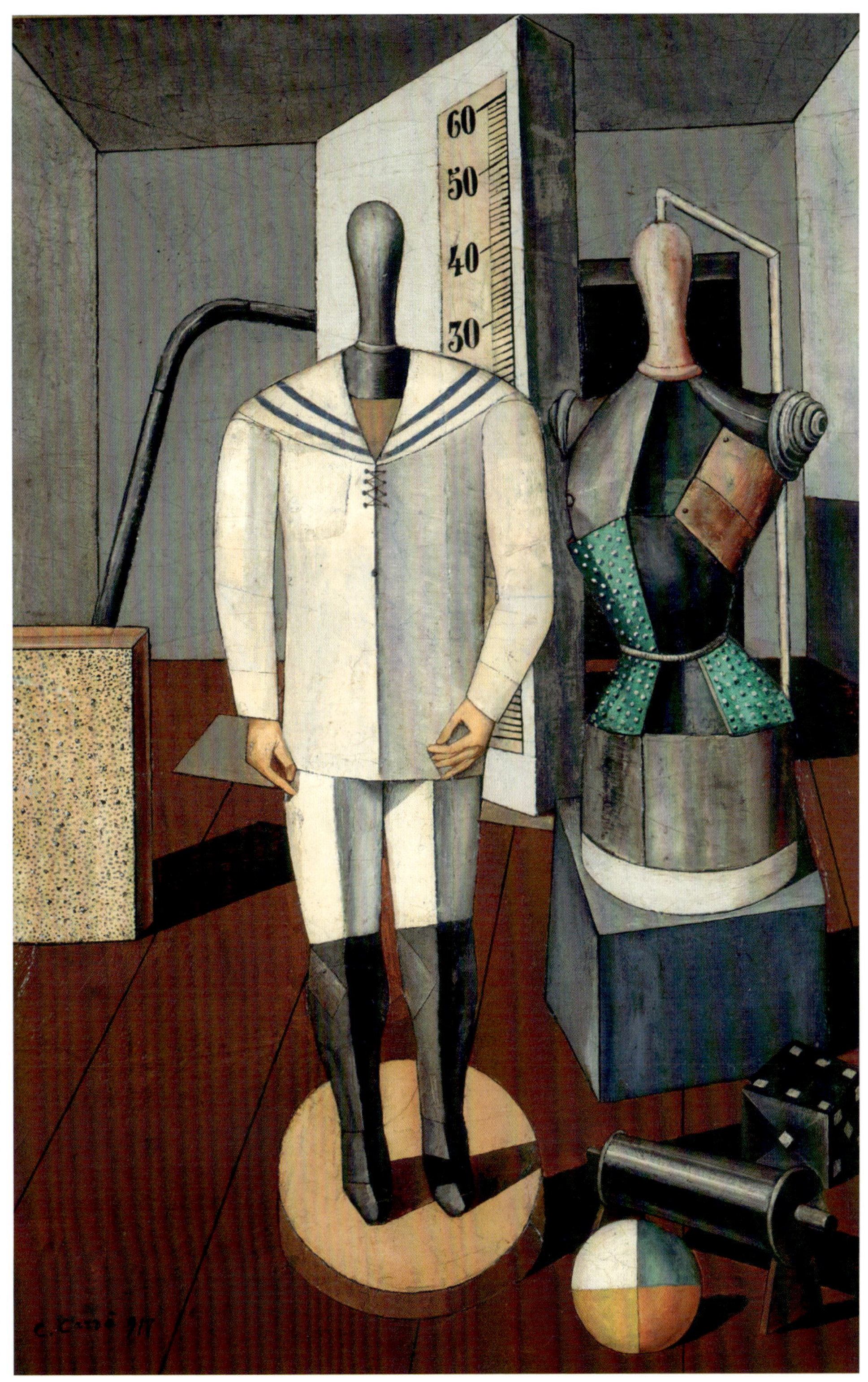

Carlo Carrà
Mother and Son, 1917
Oil on canvas, 90 x 59.5 cm

This painting – executed in the autumn of 1914 in Paris, where the artist lived from 1911 – was left unfinished because of de Chirico's sudden return home in May 1915 when Italy entered the First World War.

The work has an extremely interesting experimental quality, revealing the formal and inventive processes of the artist at a decisive moment in the development of Metaphysical painting. The focal point of the work is a female figure typical of Arnold Böcklin's imagery – a painter much admired by de Chirico – which represents a variation on the antique statues found in other paintings by the artist from around the same time. The composition proposes a series of 'objects of memory' – the brick wall, the crenellated cylindrical tower, the geometric forms, the painting within the paining – developed according to the aesthetics of the enigma and irony outlined by the artist in his writings of 1919. The work was possibly backdated either by de Chirico himself, or by Paul Guillaume, the famous collector who bought the painting in 1918. After appearing on the Parisian market, and subsequently at auction houses in London and Italy, the work was purchased by a private collector in 1998.

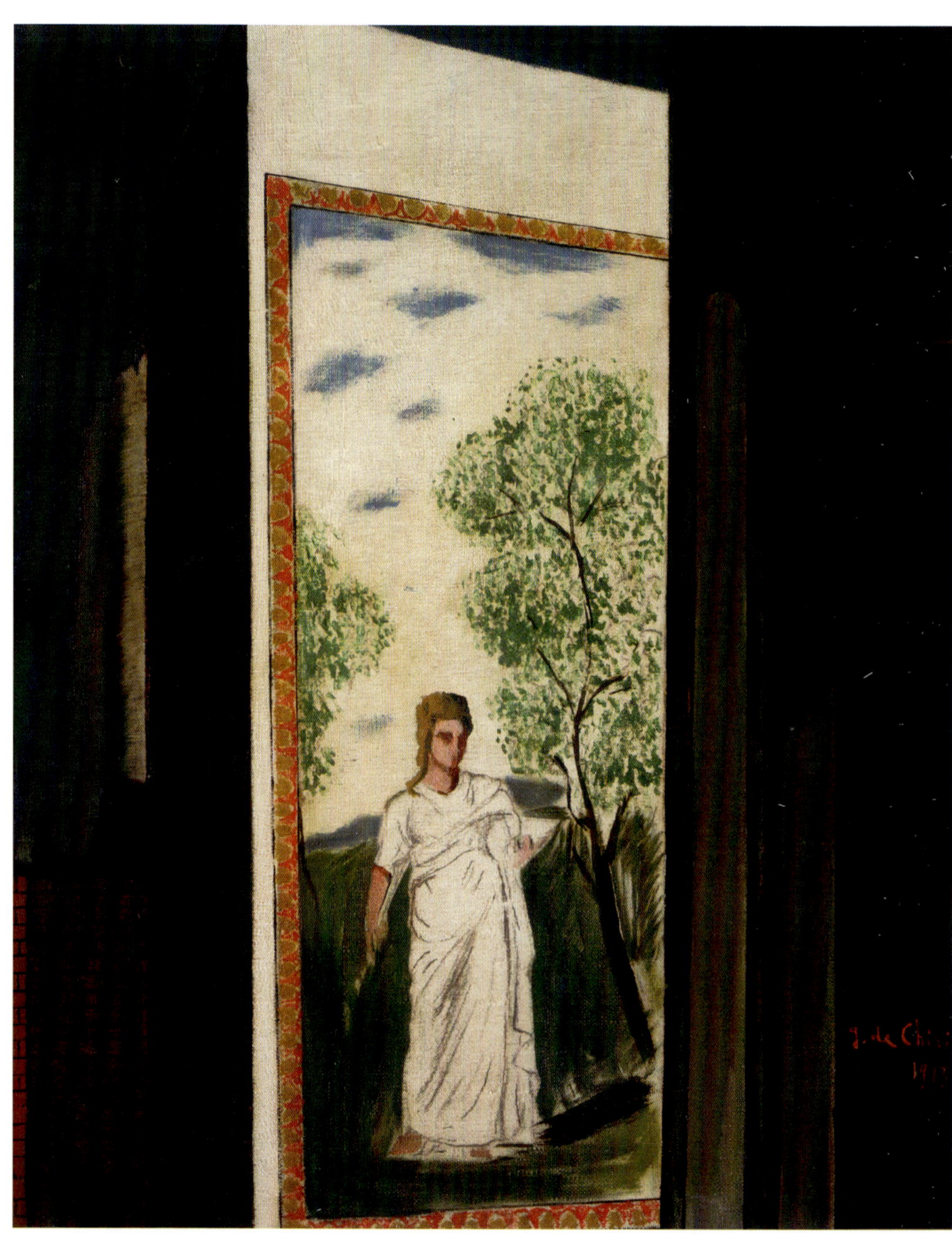

Giorgio de Chirico
Le printemps de l'ingénieur, 1914
(The Engineer's Springtime)
Oil on canvas, 52 x 43 cm

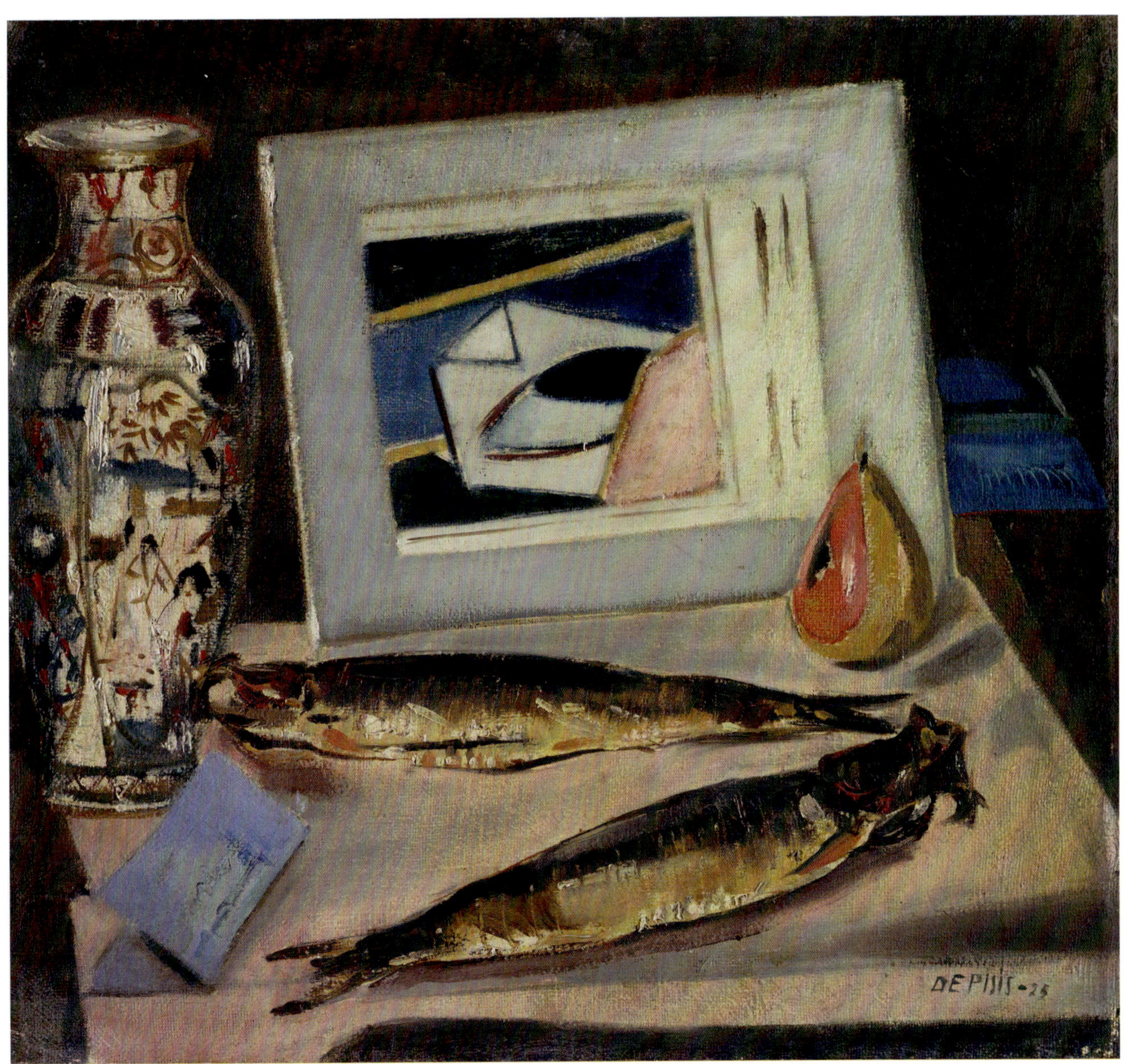

Filippo de Pisis
Sacred Fish, 1925
Oil on canvas, 55 x 62.5 cm

Born Luigi Filippo Tibertelli, de Pisis cultivated many interests ranging from botany to the history of art, and from painting to literature. In fact, he started out as a poet, and wrote verse influenced by the imagery of Giorgio de Chirico, who he met in Ferrara during the First World War. After moving to Rome in 1919, he established links with the Valori Plastici group and turned his attention to painting.

Sacred Fish contains references to the art and iconography of both de Chirico and Giorgio Morandi, in addition to objects typical of the painter's own vocabulary, such as the Chinese vase and the folded sheet of paper.

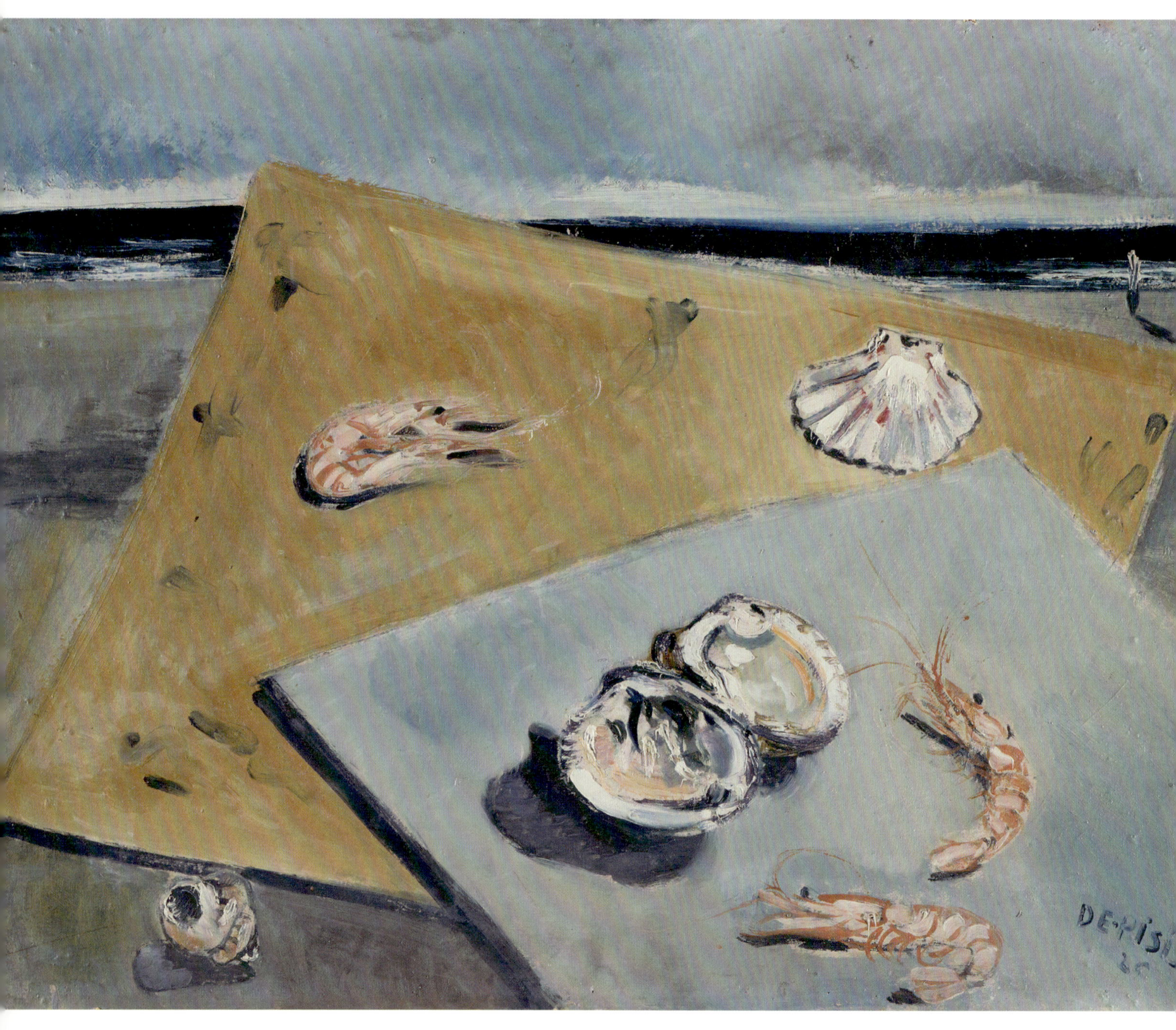

Filippo de Pisis
Marine Still Life with Shrimps, 1926
Oil on card, 52 x 68 cm

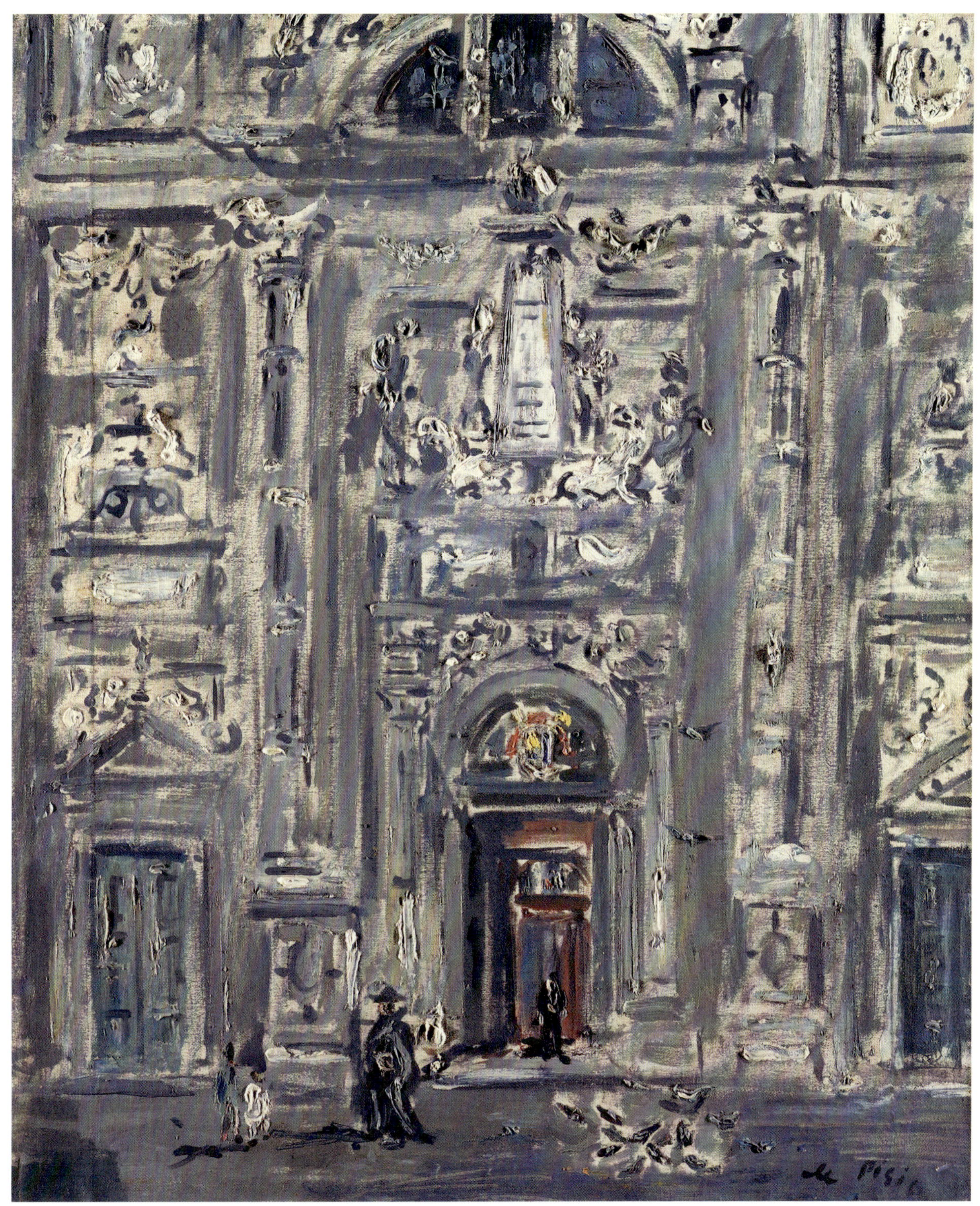

Filippo de Pisis
Perspectival View of a Venetian Church (San Moisè), 1930
Oil on canvas, 81 x 67 cm

In 1925, de Pisis moved to Paris and his work began to focus on the study of light and colour, whilst retaining the enigmatic qualities of his earlier Metaphysical atmospheres. Such concerns – treated in an impressionist manner – are also evident in his painting of the façade of San Moisè in Venice, rendered with an intricate network of feverish brushstrokes.

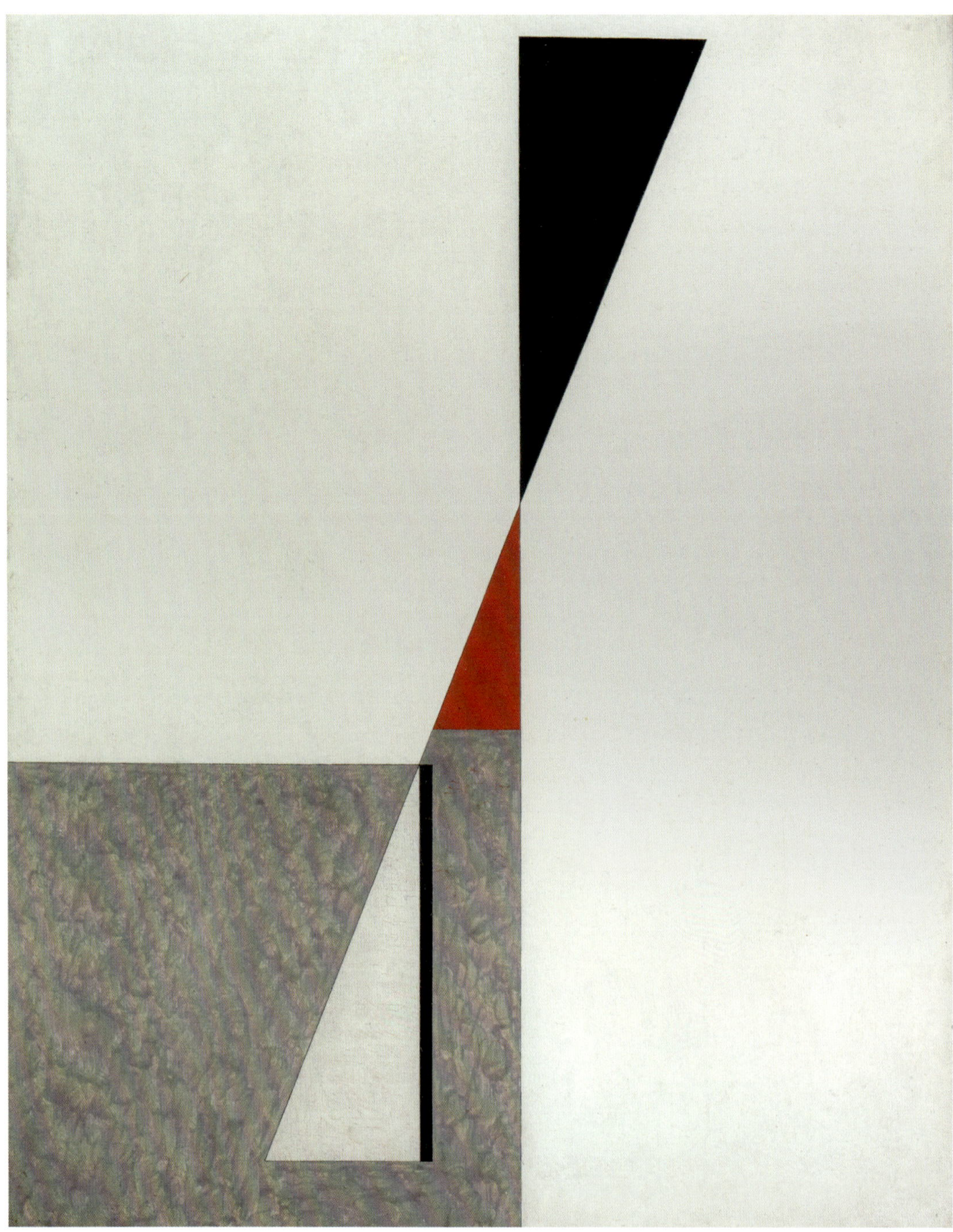

Osvaldo Licini
Equilibrium, 1934
Oil on canvas, 90 x 67.2 cm

Licini abandoned figurative painting around 1930 following his encounter with the Parisian Circle et Carré and Abstraction-Création groups. *Equilibrium* explores the artist's belief that "geometry can become feeling". It was exhibited at the 1935 Rome Quadriennale alongside paintings by Lucio Fontana and other artists who gravitated around Milan's Il Milione gallery, providing him with an opportunity to establish links with the main representatives of Italian abstractionism.

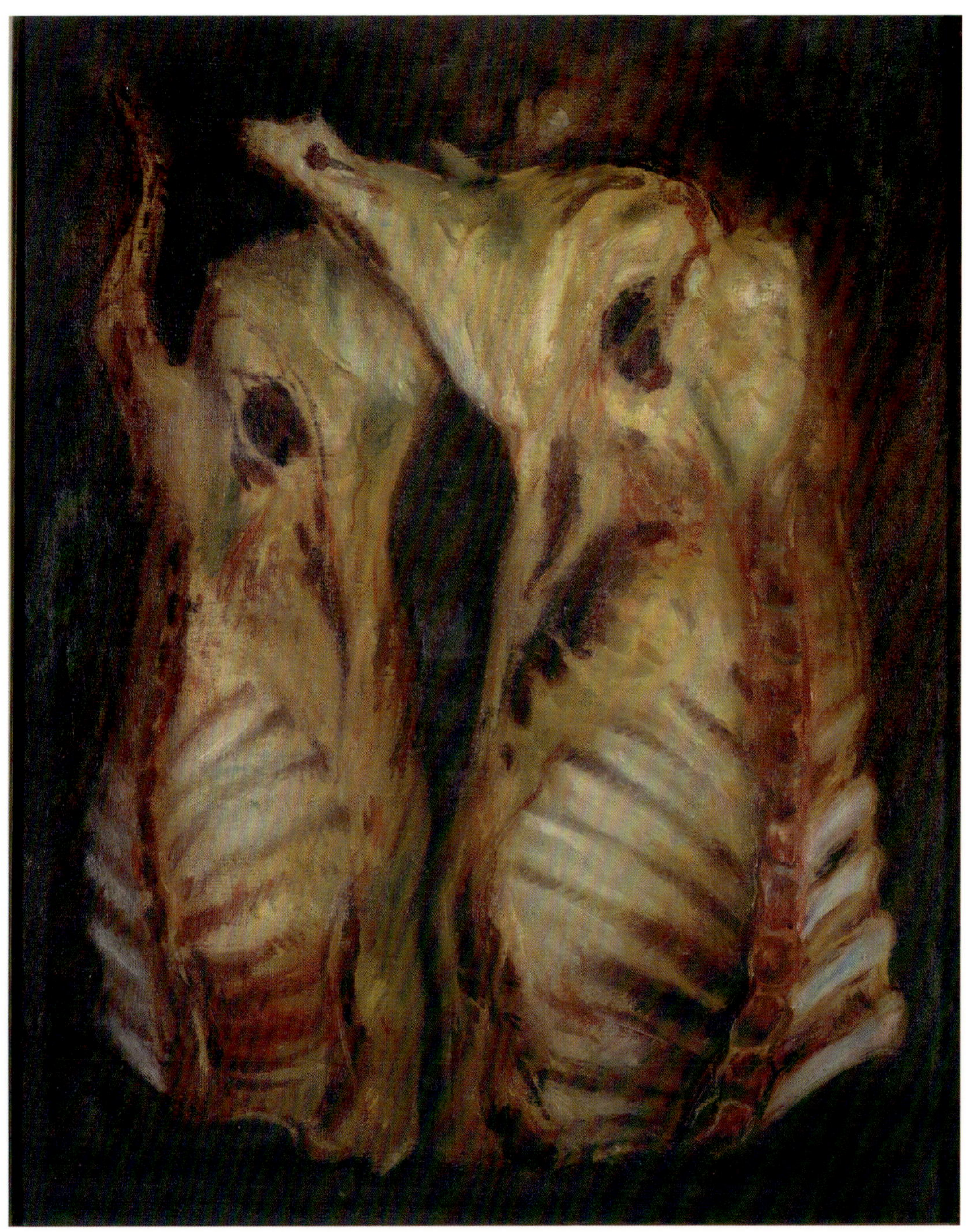

Mario Mafai
Butchered Ox, 1930
Oil on canvas,
116 x 93.5 cm

Mafai studied at the Academy of Fine Arts in Rome, and during the late 1920s was one of the founding members of the Scuola romana, alongside his friend Scipione and Marino Mazzacurati. *Butchered Ox* epitomises the intensely expressive and emotional painterly style developed by the group.

By contrast, *Dried Flowers* (p. 26) is an essential and almost graphic work, its rarefied forms marking a new, more lyrical and contemplative phase following his expressionist period.

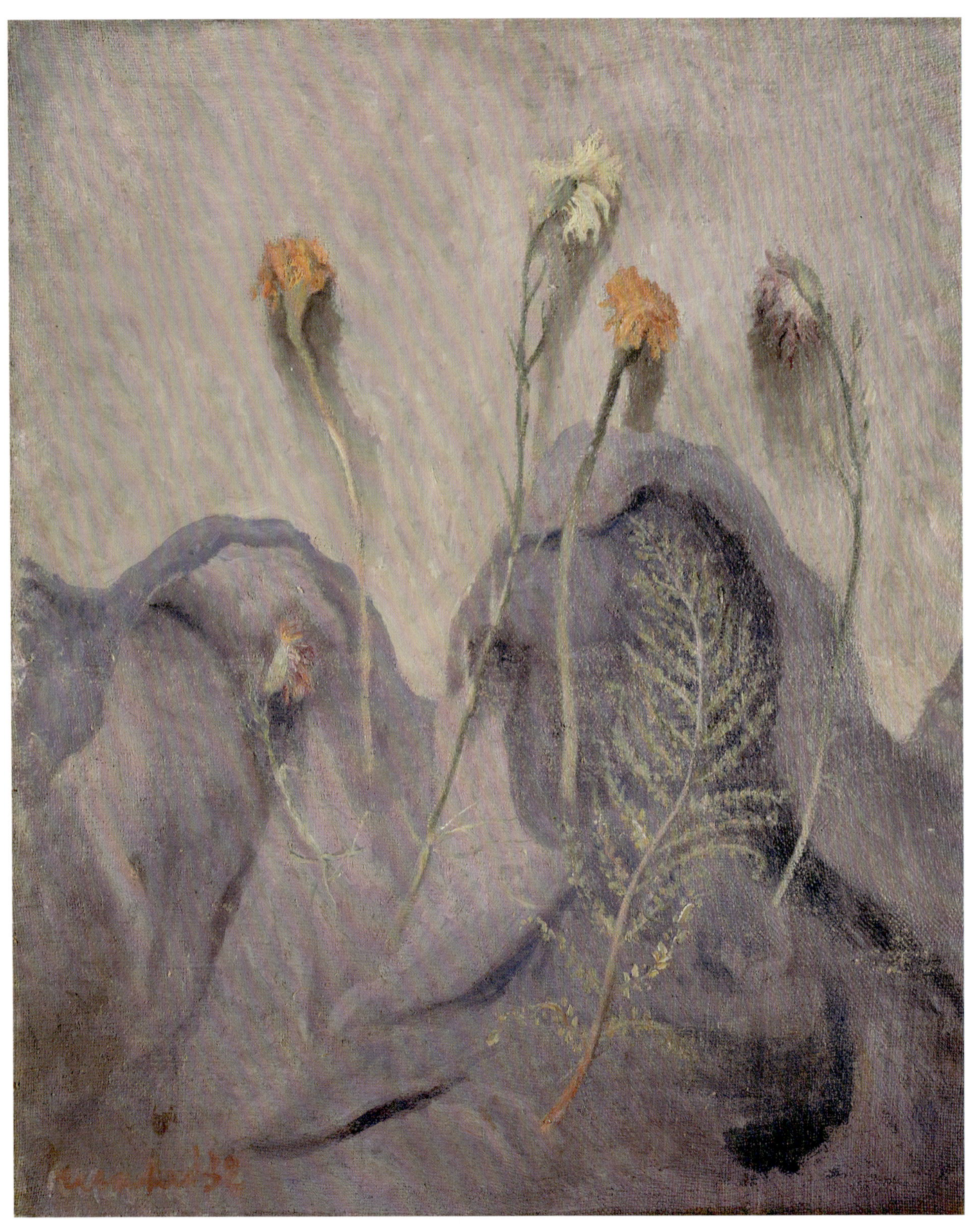

Mario Mafai
Dried Flowers, 1932
Oil on canvas, 61.5 x 50 cm

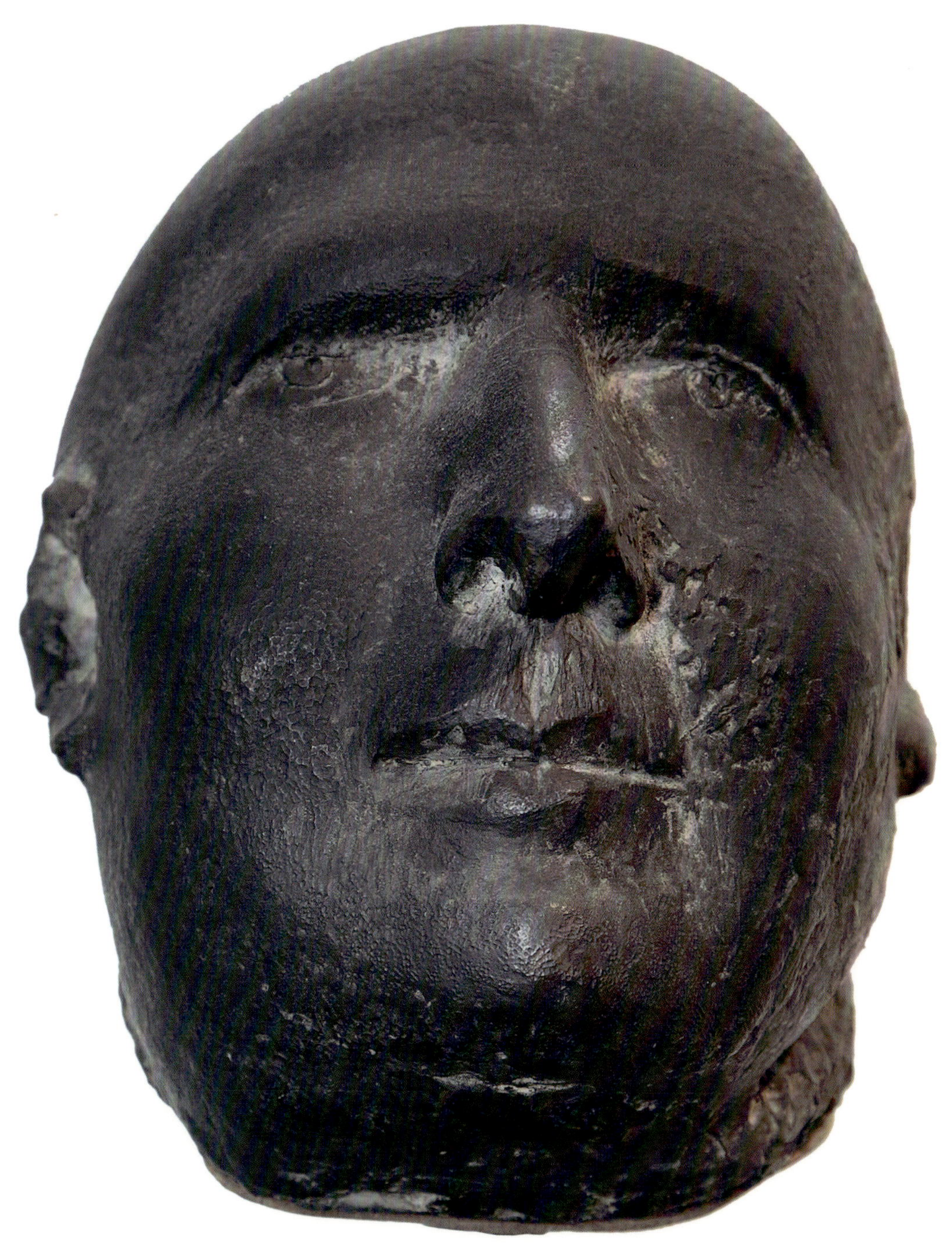

Marino Marini
Portrait of Emilio Jesi, 1947
Bronze, 22 x 20 x 23 cm

Emilio Jesi was undoubtedly the most important collector of Marini's work, and was one of the artist's patrons to be portrayed during these years in works of a surprising stylistic variety that resulted from Marini's will to express the individual 'poetry' in every human face. The original plaster version of this work was exhibited at the 1948 Venice Biennale.

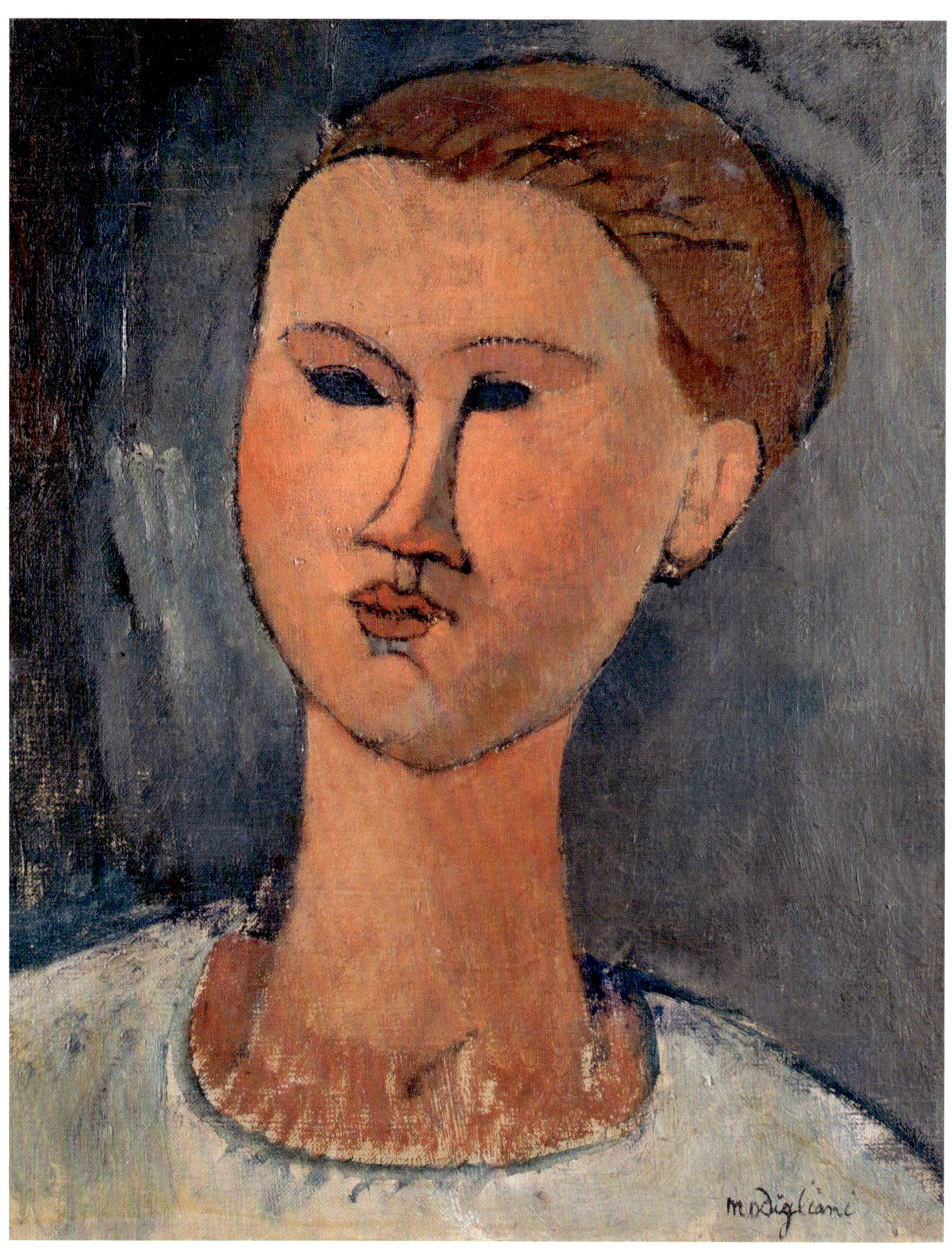

Amedeo Modigliani
Head of a Young Woman, 1915
Oil on canvas, 46 x 38 cm

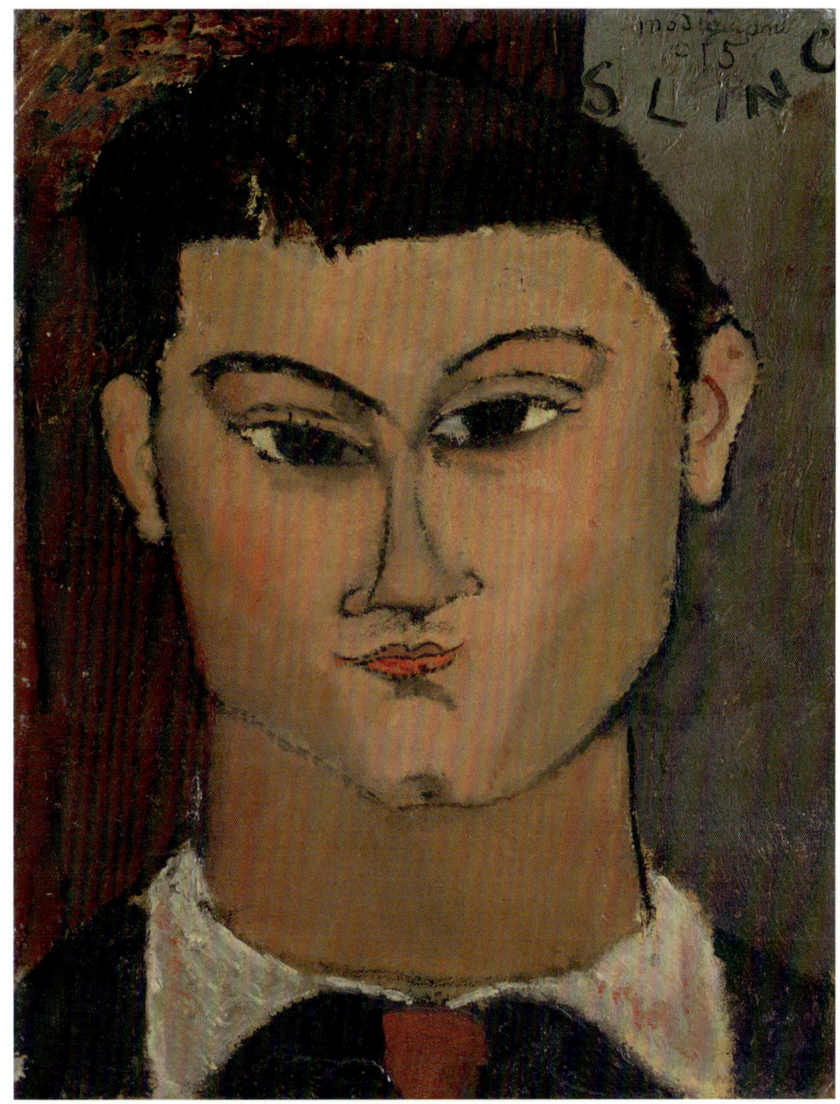

Modigliani moved permanently to Paris in 1906, where he became associated with the avant-garde circles around Guillaume Apollinaire. The majority of his works were created between 1915 and 1918, and consisted of portraits of friends belonging to his bohemian milieu. *Head of a Young Woman* probably portrays the English writer Beatrice Hastings with whom Modigliani had a tumultuous relationship.

This work, together with the *Portrait of Moïse Kisling*, previously belonged to Paul Guillaume, an art critic and merchant who was the first – and for a time, only – figure to appreciate and collect Modigliani's work. Both paintings arrived in Italy after the incredible success of the artist's retrospective at the 1930 Venice Biennale, and were purchased by the Il Milione gallery in Milan; they entered Emilio Jesi's collection in the immediate post-war period.

Amedeo Modigliani
Portrait of Moïse Kisling, 1915
Oil on canvas, 37 x 29 cm

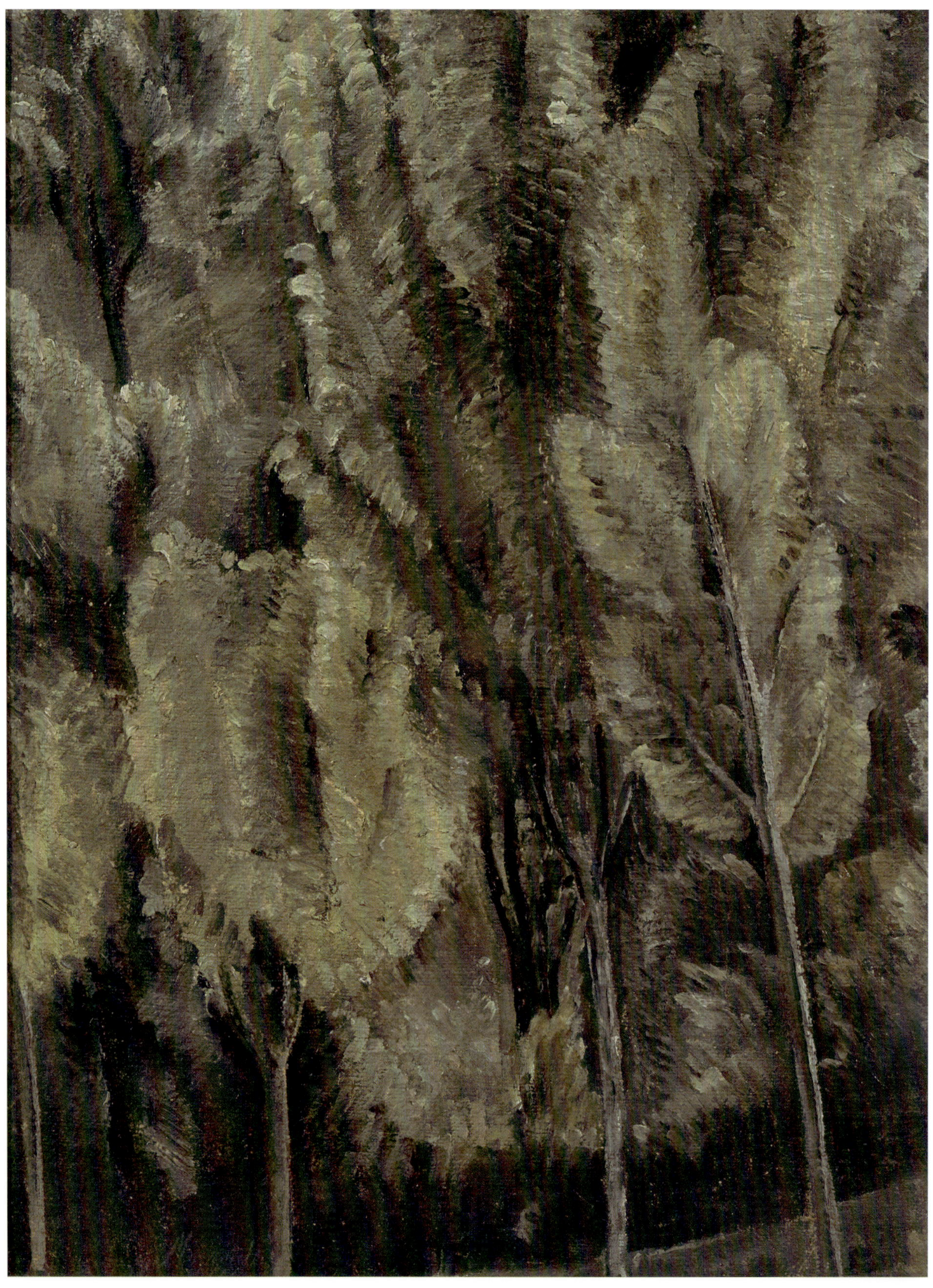

Giorgio Morandi is represented in the Jesi Collection by an extraordinary series of landscapes and still lifes that form an anthology of masterpieces, documenting the various stages in the painter's career.

An unusual, solitary figure who never left the city of his birth and – with rare exceptions – only knew the work of his contemporaries from books, Morandi pursued a highly personal artistic vision throughout his life. His images focused on a few humble subjects and were characterised by intellectual enquiry, extreme purity of expression and absolute rigor of form. He stood aloof from the revolutionary clamor of the avant-gardes, yet was interested (in a wholly personal way) in the ideas of Futurism, Valori Plastici and the Novecento school. Around 1918, the reproductions published in the Bolognese magazine *La Raccolta* also drew Morandi's attention to the Metaphysical research of Giorgio de Chirico and Carlo Carrà.

Like the *Landscape* of 1916, *The Wood* belongs to the years of Morandi's discovery of Cézanne, Henry Rousseau and Cubism. In the latter, a grey-green curtain of tall trees sways in the wind, and no figures, buildings or other visual elements break into the crowded space.

From the twenties onward, Morandi devoted himself exclusively to investigating the relationships between objects, to studying space and volume, and to capturing the shifting light of the landscape. These concerns are typified in works such as *Still Life* (p. 34), which Emilio Jesi purchased directly from the artist, as well as *Landscape (The Pink House)*.

Giorgio Morandi
Landscape (The Wood), 1914
Oil on canvas, 60 x 45 cm

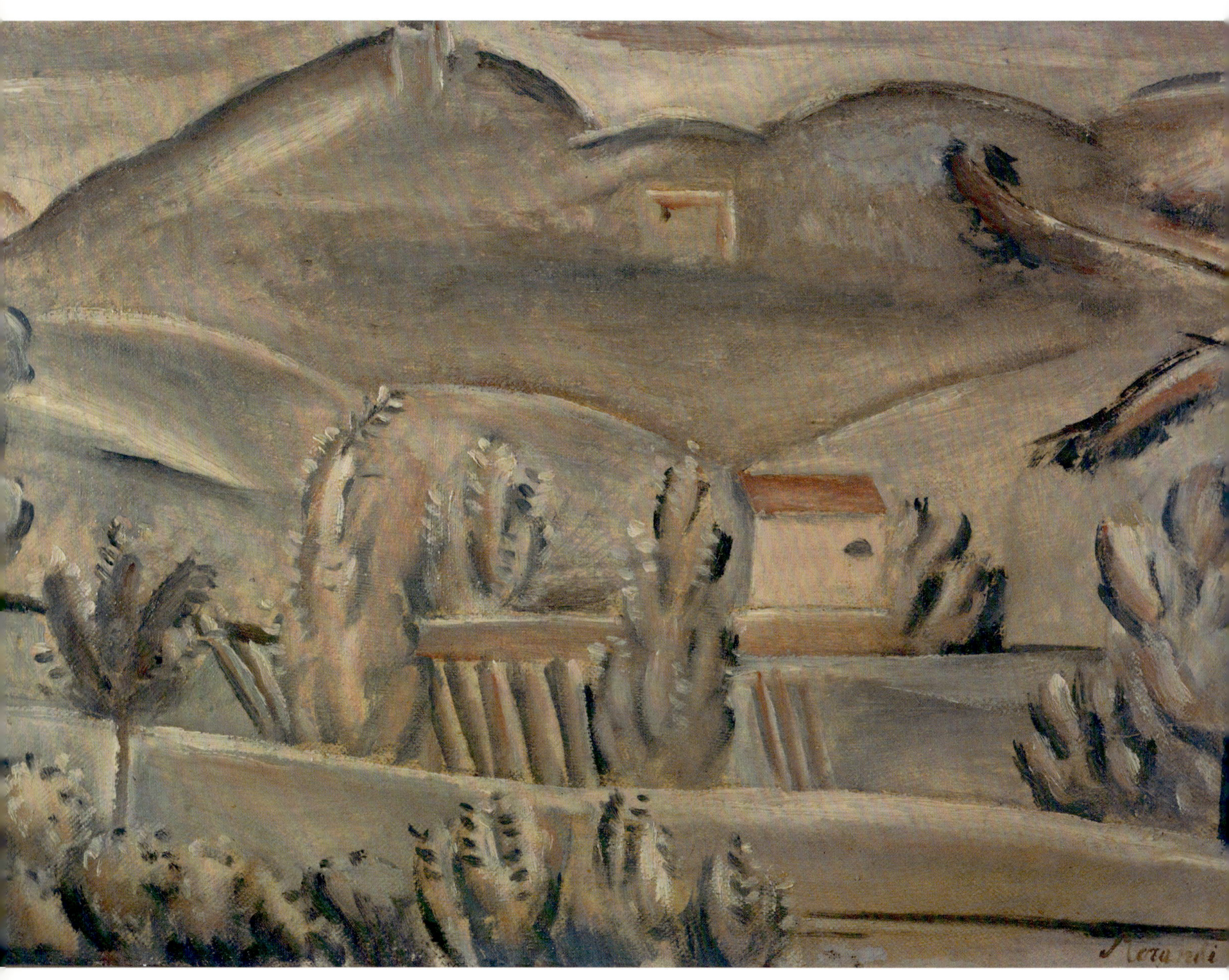

Giorgio Morandi
Landscape, 1916
Oil on canvas, 39 x 54 cm

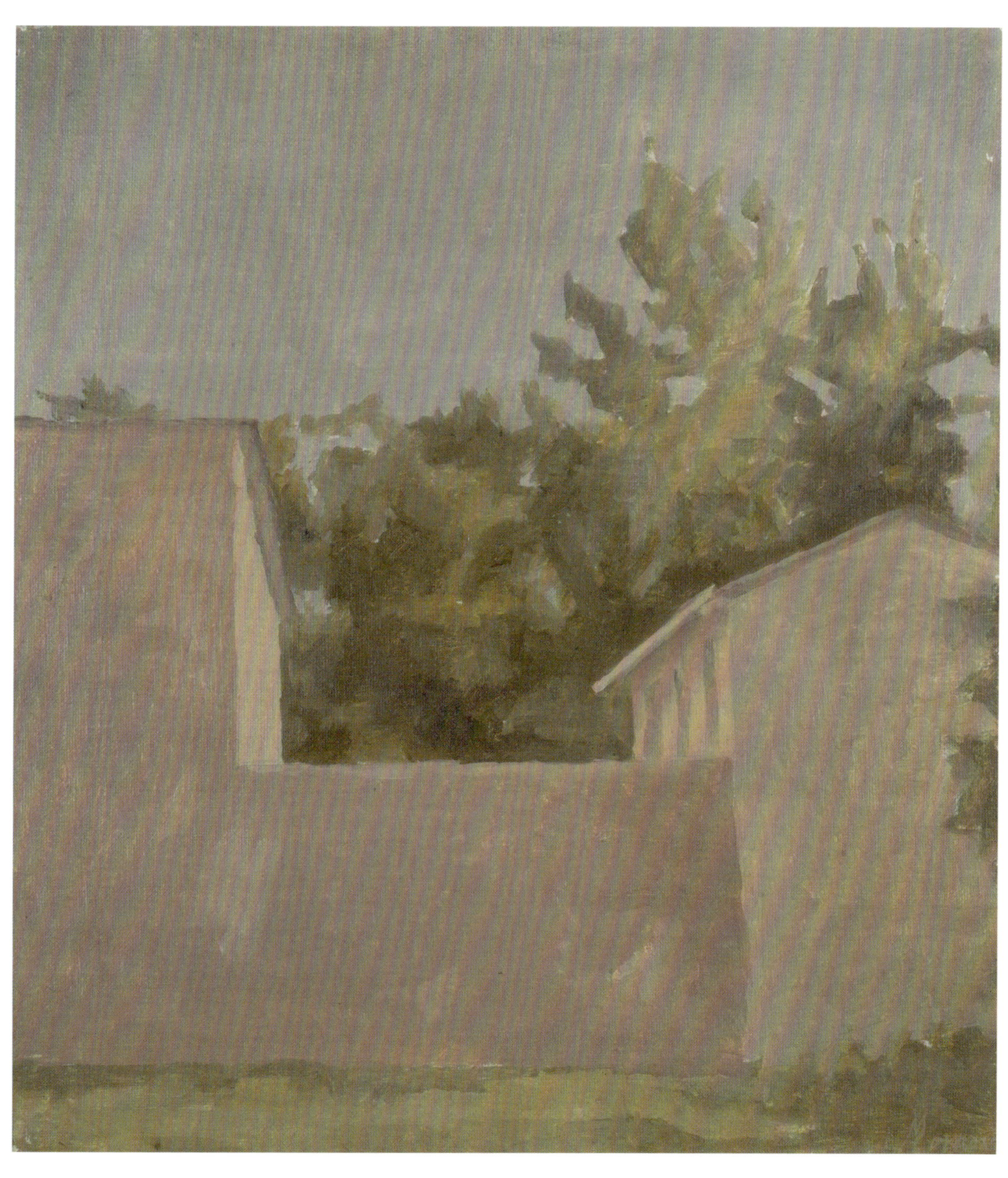

Giorgio Morandi
Landscape (The Pink House), 1925
Oil on canvas, 46 x 42 cm

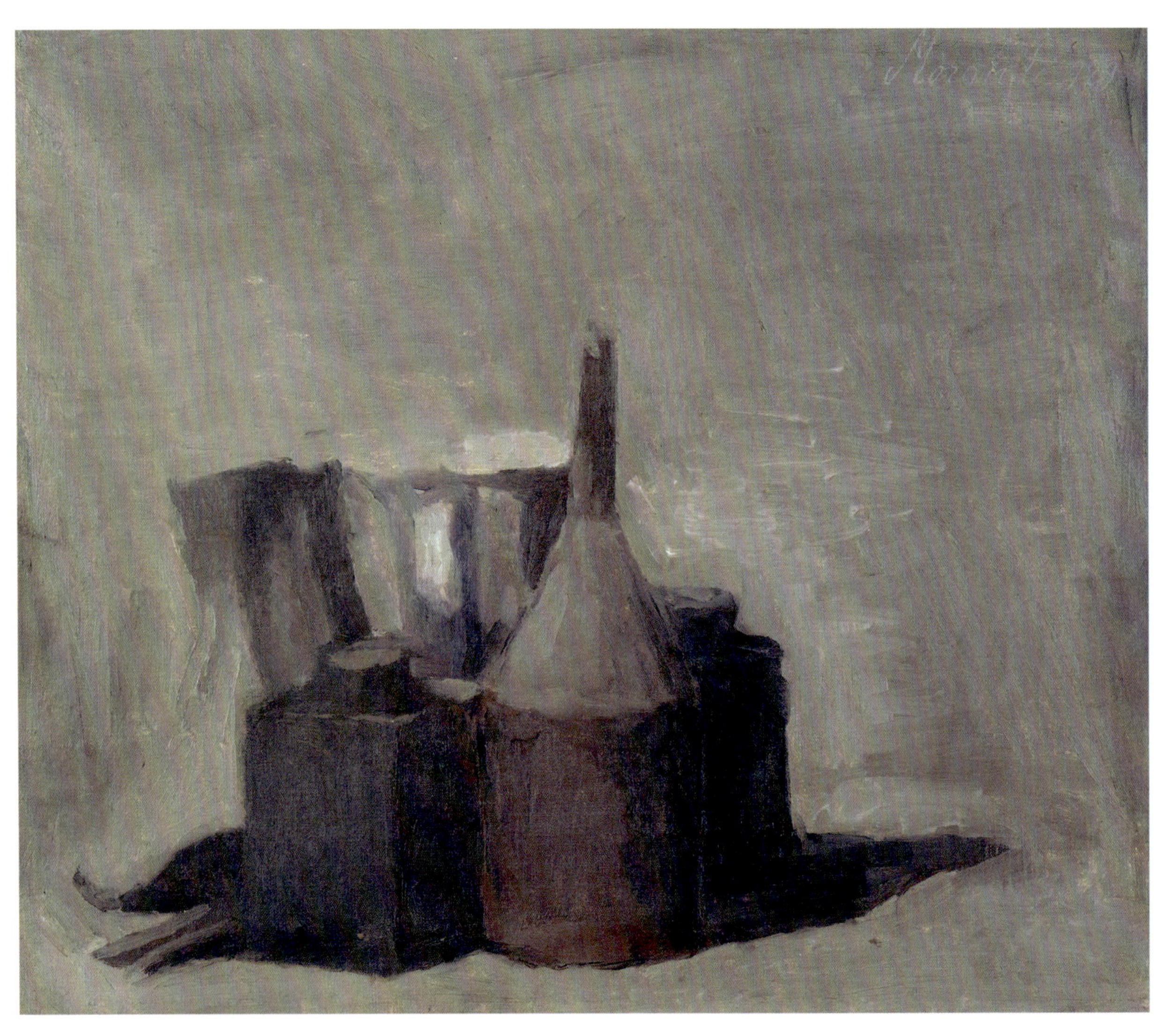

Giorgio Morandi
Still Life, 1929
Oil on canvas, 55 x 58 cm

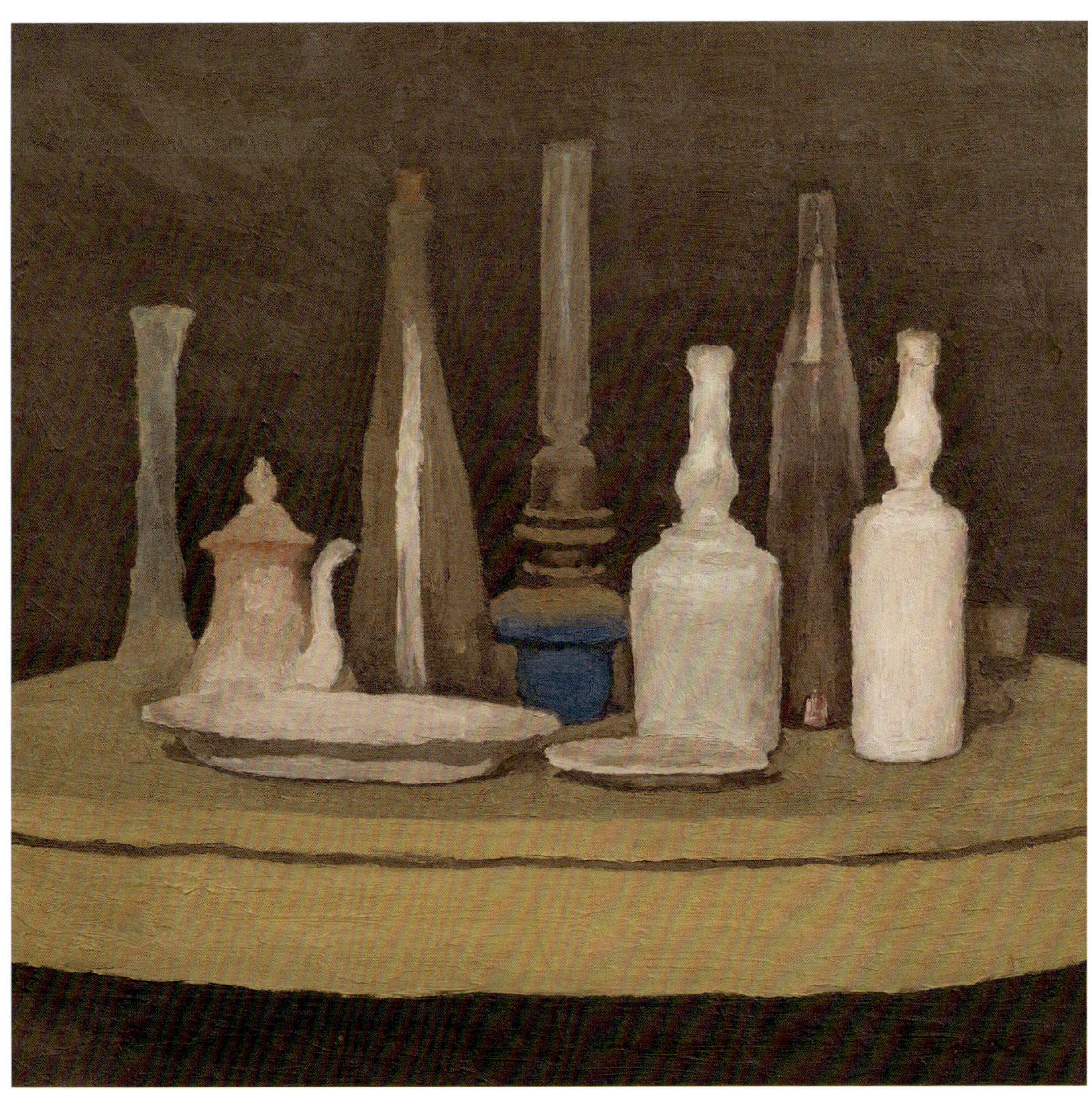

Giorgio Morandi
Still Life, 1929
Oil on canvas, 50 x 60 cm

This work – "populated not by things but by the ghosts of things",
according to Lamberto Vitali's famous description – entered the
Pinacoteca in 1976 as part of the first Jesi donation. Emilio Jesi bought
it in 1939 from Luigi Bartolini, an artist, engraver and writer who was
initially a friend of Morandi's but later one of his fiercest detractors.
Cesare Brandi described the work as "truly stupendous: it takes
your breath away with those nocturnal blues and those sandy tones,
vibrating like a sustained note".

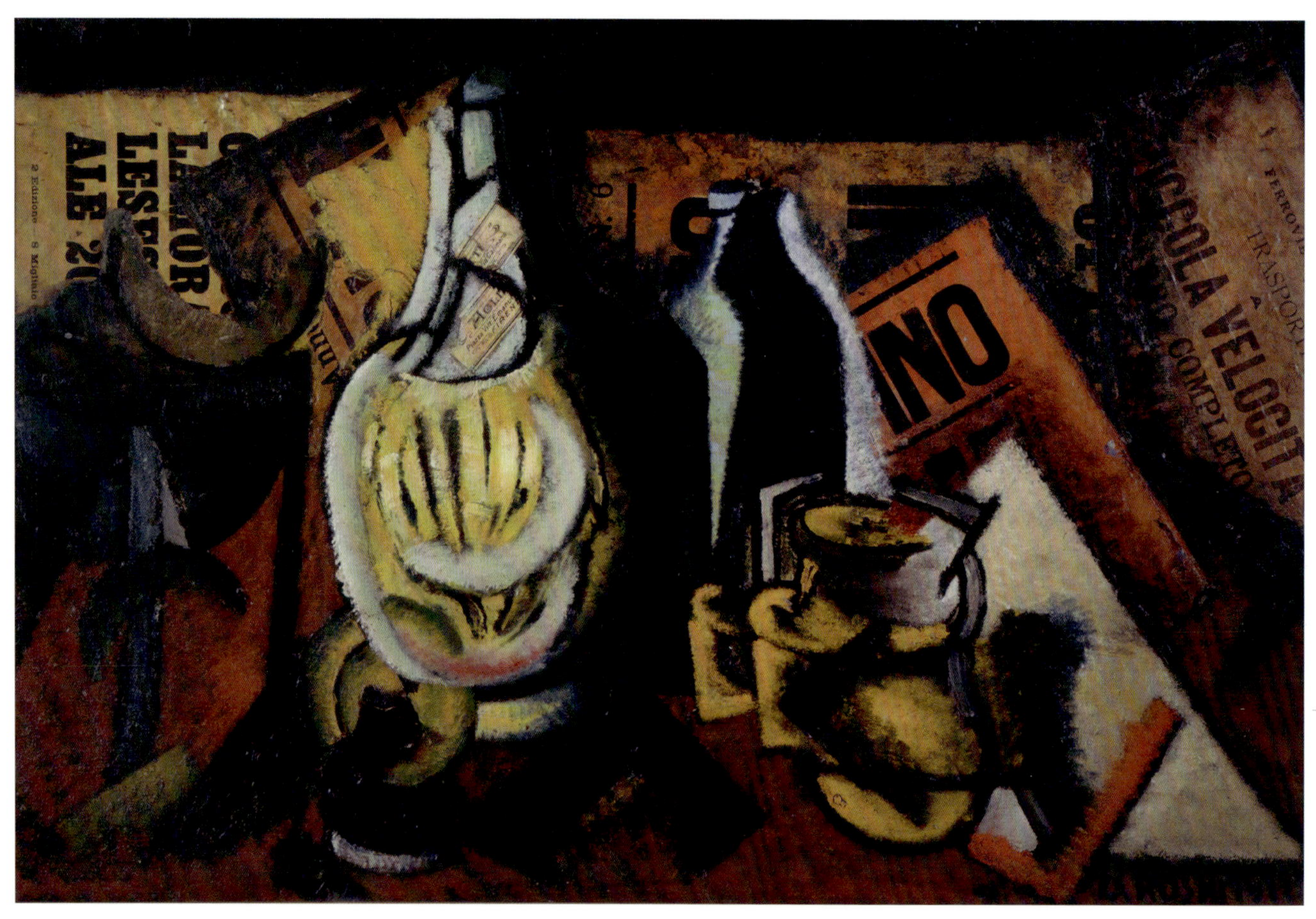

Ottone Rosai
Still Life: The Carpenter's Bench, 1914
Oil and collage on card, 45.5 x 70 cm

During the early years of his artistic training Rosai was fascinated
by French painting, particularly artists such as Courbet, Daumier
and Cézanne. Corot was a major influence on the works exhibited
in his first solo exhibition of 1913. However, that year Rosai
met Ardengo Soffici and was drawn into the Futurist movement
for a brief time. This work is typical of the dynamic imagery he
produced as a member of the group, inspired by the collage
aesthetic that was then almost as popular among Futurist artists as
it was with the Cubists.

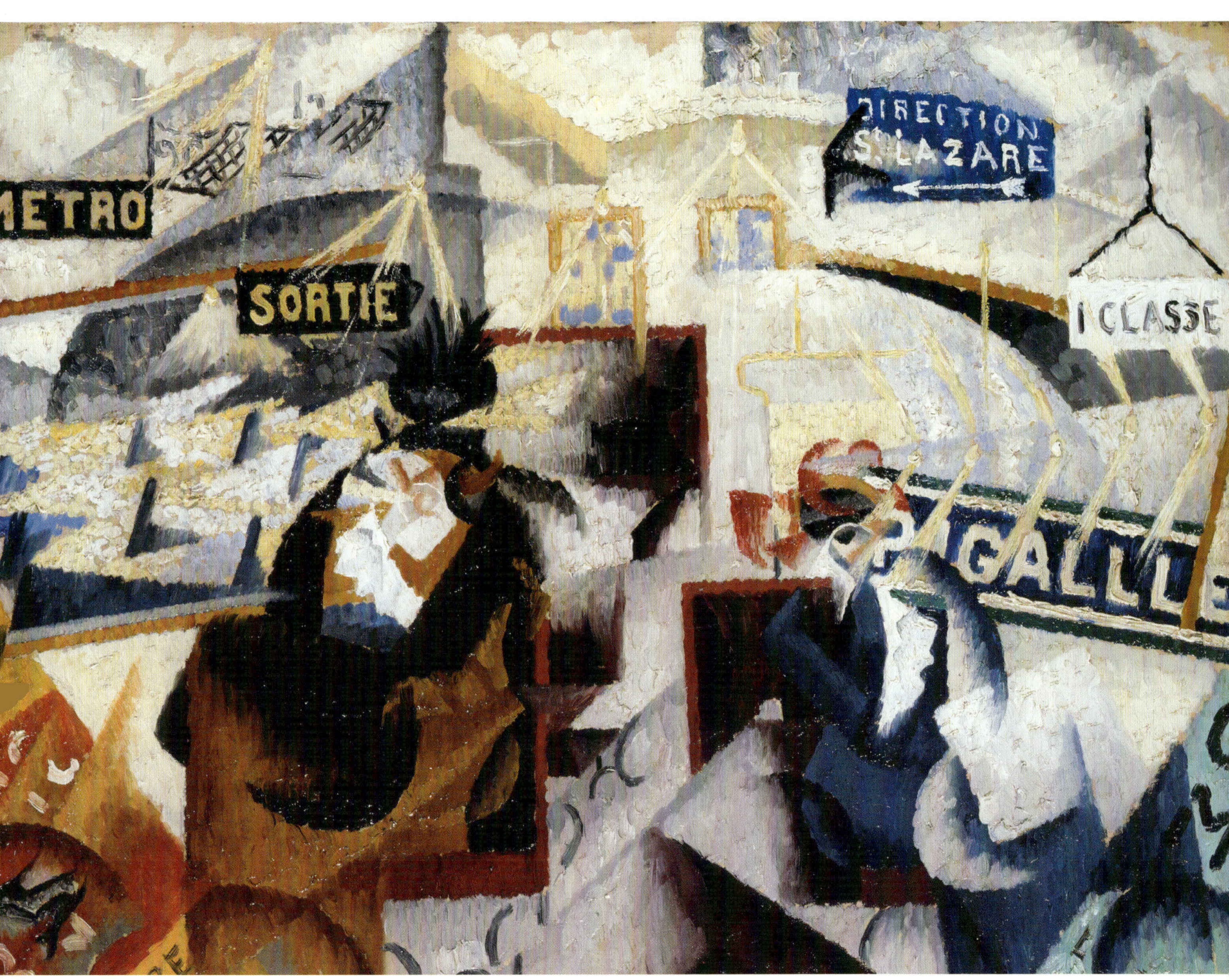

Gino Severini
Le Nord-Sud, 1912
Oil on board, 49 x 64 cm

After working alongside Umberto Boccioni and the Divisionist painters who gravitated toward Giacomo Balla's Roman studio, Severini moved to Paris in 1906. He joined the Futurist movement four years later, developing a singular interpretation of its principles. *Le Nord-Sud* addresses the typically Futurist theme of the 'simultaneous view', whereby a number of different scenes or motifs are compressed into a single image in order to convey the fleeting, confused sensations received in the modern urban environment – in this specific case, while travelling on the Paris Métro.

Moving away from Futurism after the First World War, Severini
began to develop a new style based on the formal rigour of Synthetic
Cubism. This approach, which was to become increasingly informed
by mathematical principles, is represented here by *Large Still Life with
Pumpkin* of 1917, in which the deconstruction of images theorised by
Braque and Picasso is interpreted in an essentially decorative manner.

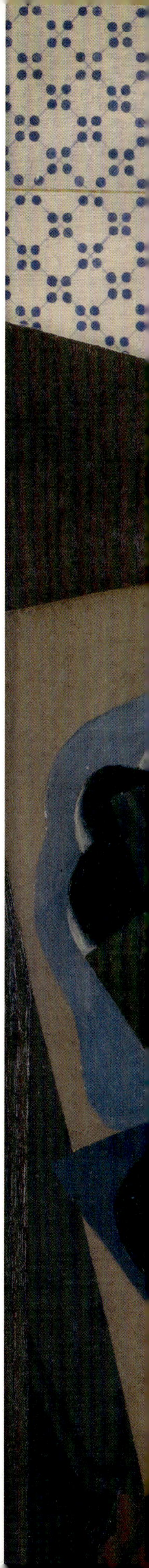

Gino Severini
Large Still Life with Pumpkin, 1917
Oil on board, 92 x 65 cm

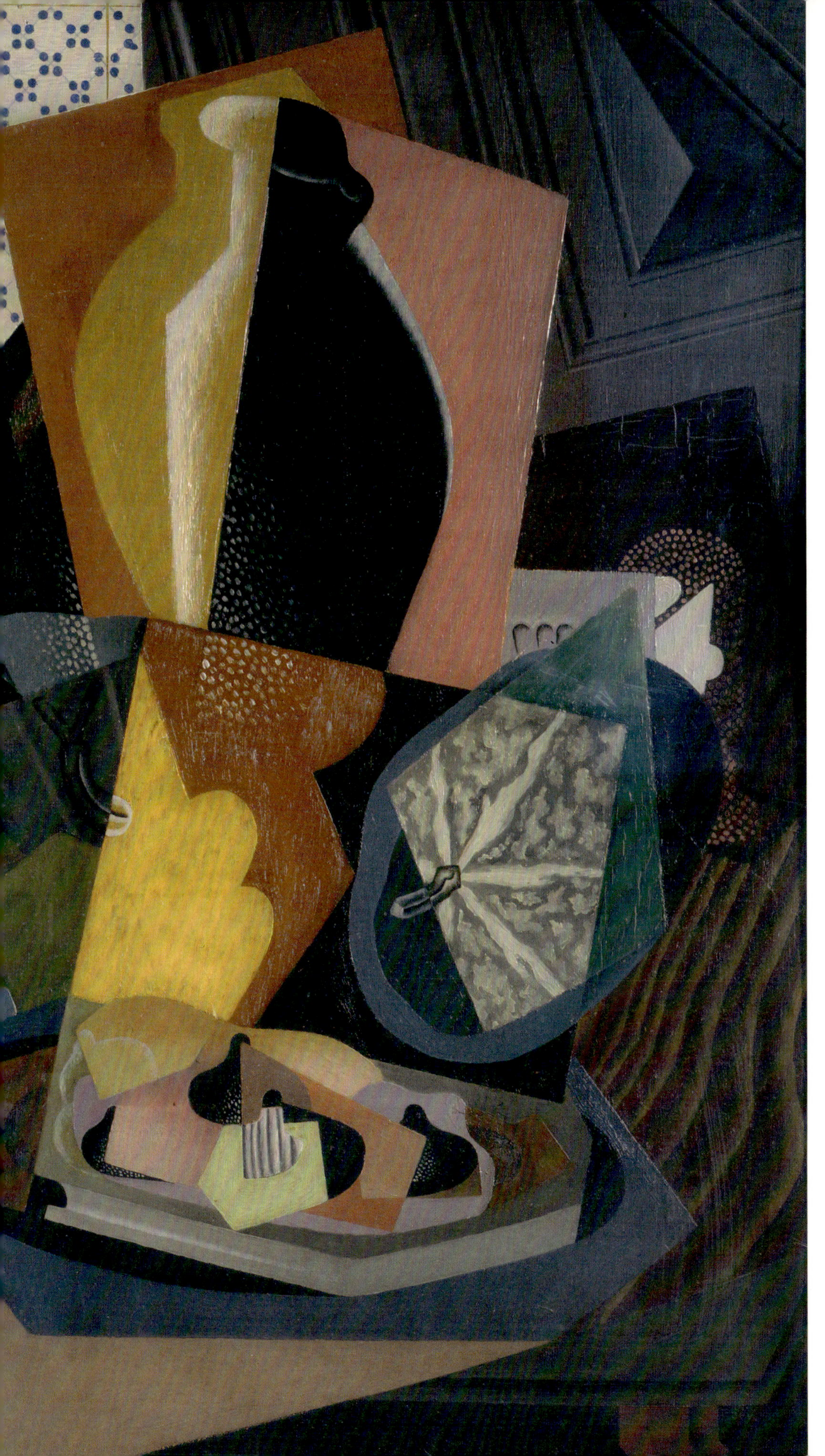

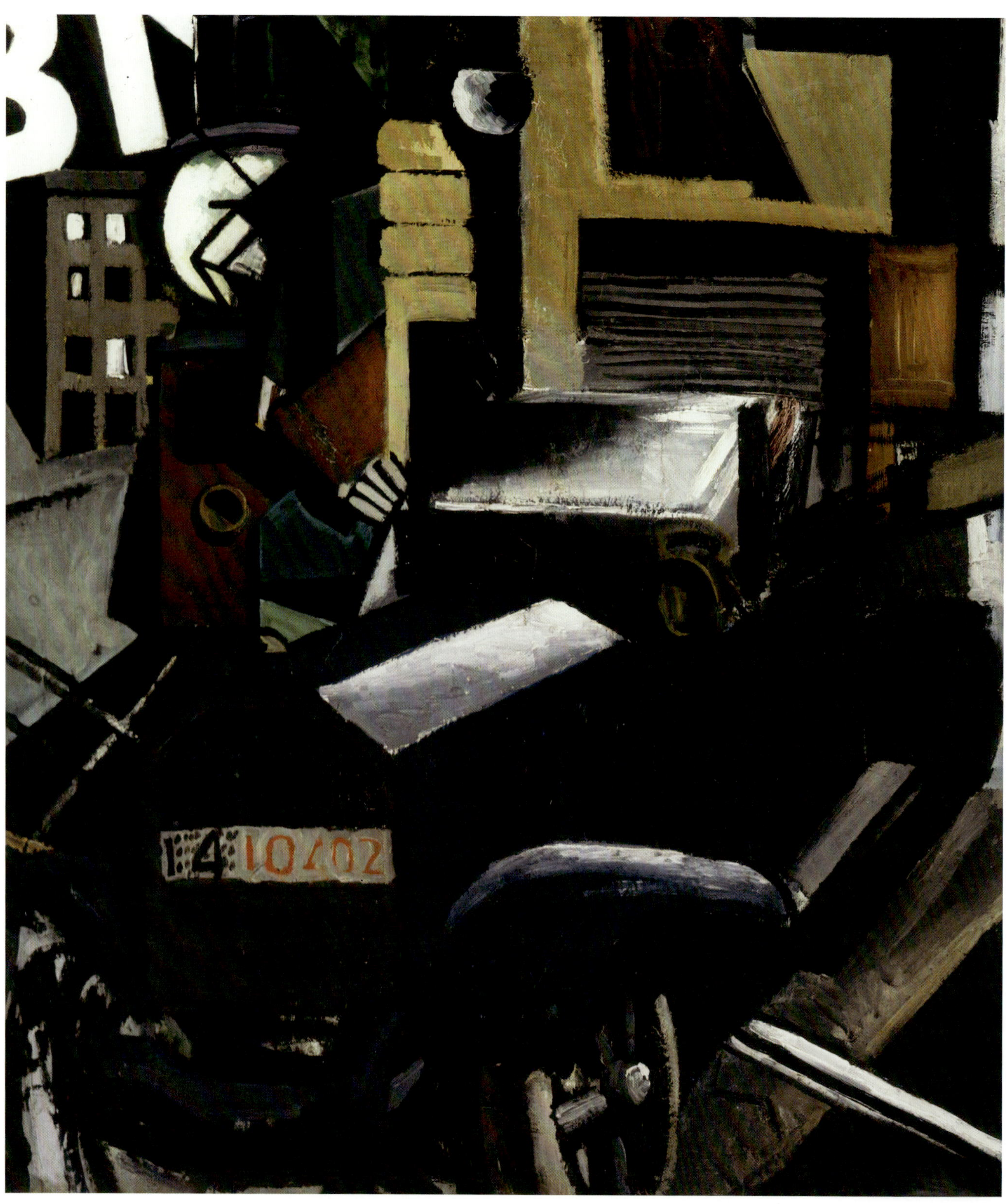

10402

The paintings by Sironi in the collection of Emilio Jesi – an anti-Fascist of Jewish ancestry – pre-date the artist's support for the 'Fascist revolution' and his involvement in the great decorative undertakings promoted by the regime, or at least are conceptually extraneous to them. Sironi abandoned his engineering studies in 1902 and began to frequent Giacomo Balla's studio in Rome, where he met Umberto Boccioni and Gino Severini. The Futurist ideas of his friends would later also enthuse him.

An example of the movement's influence on his work is *The Truck*, while *The Lamp* draws heavily on Carlo Carrà's Metaphysical iconography in its depiction of an inexpressive mannequin standing in a melancholy domestic interior. The latter image exudes a sense of existential anguish that is typical of Sironi's art. Indeed, he never shared Futurism's faith in progress or celebrated the 'myth of the machine', his urban landscapes of the immediate post-war years being empty, gloomy and infused with a marked sense of alienation.

In 1922 Sironi was an important figure in the establishment of the Novecento school, an artistic tendency that set out to promote a forward-looking art that did not disdain the cultural achievements of the past. His political sympath*ies* for Mussolini – who gained power the same year – saw him go on to become an important illustrator and graphic designer for the Fascist newspaper *Il Popolo d'Italia*.

Mario Sironi
The Truck, 1914-15
Oil on card laid on canvas, 90 x 80 cm

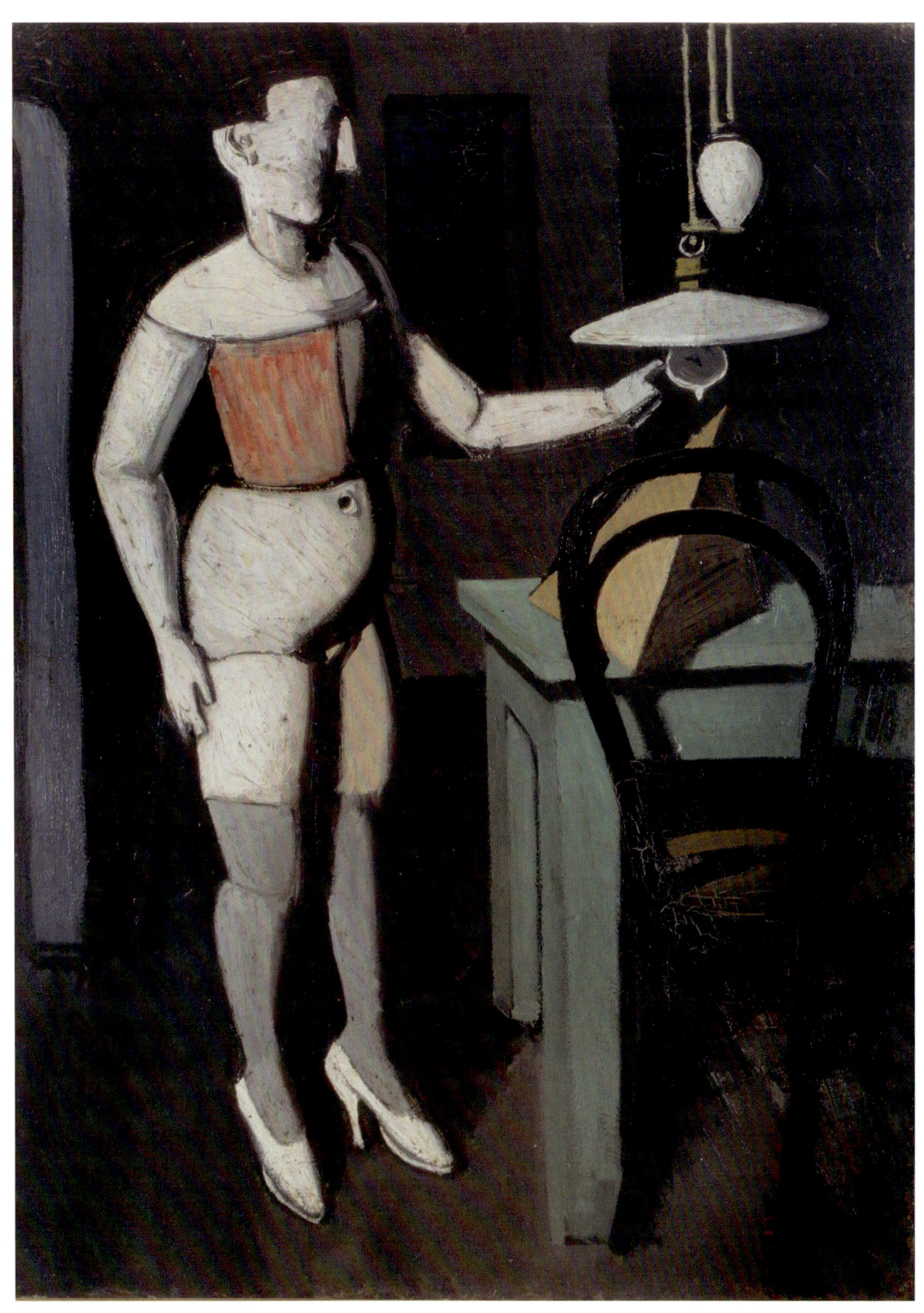

Mario Sironi
The Lamp, 1919
Oil on paper laid on canvas, 78 x 56 cm

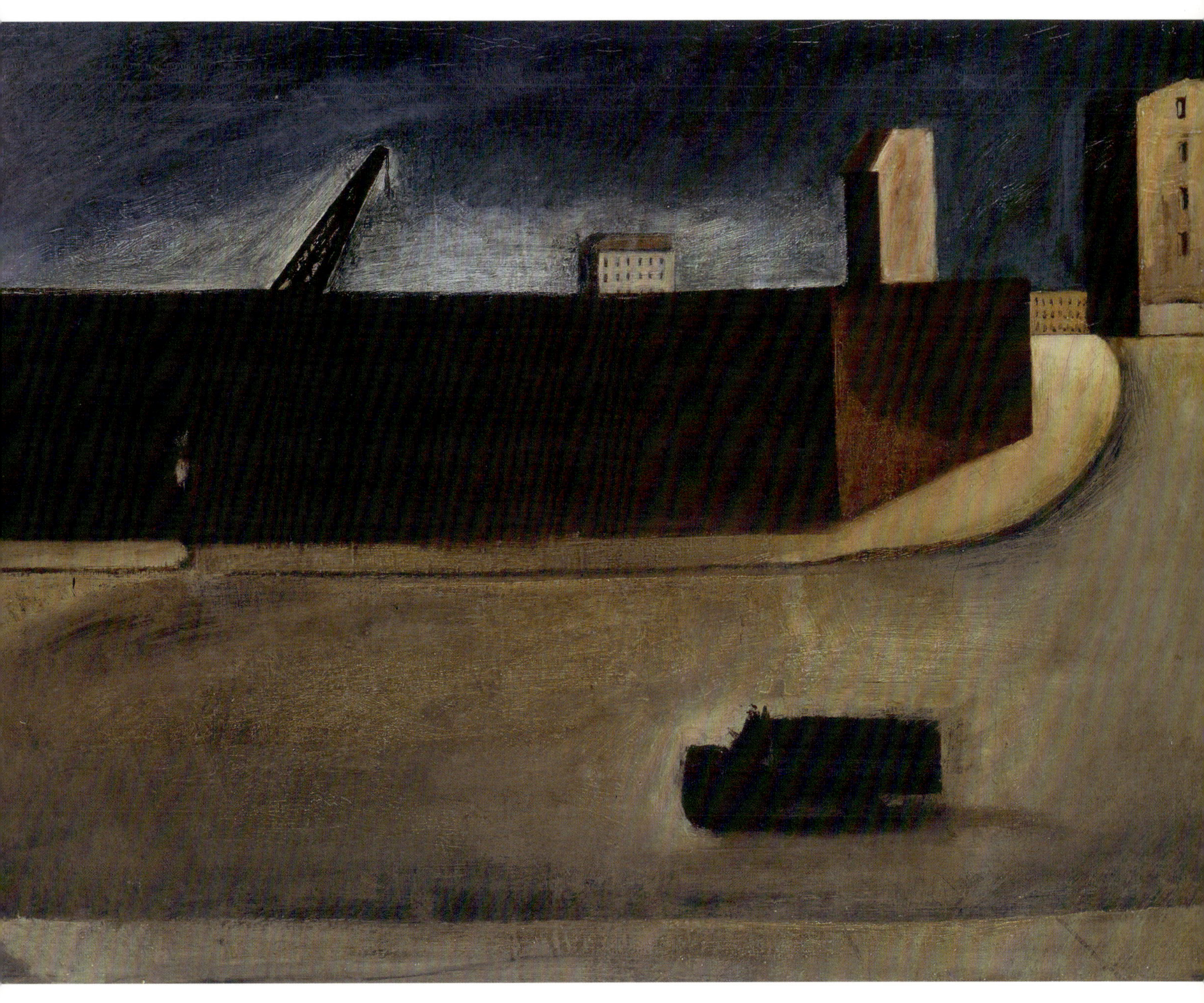

Mario Sironi
Urban Landscape with Truck, 1919-20
Oil on canvas, 44 x 60 cm

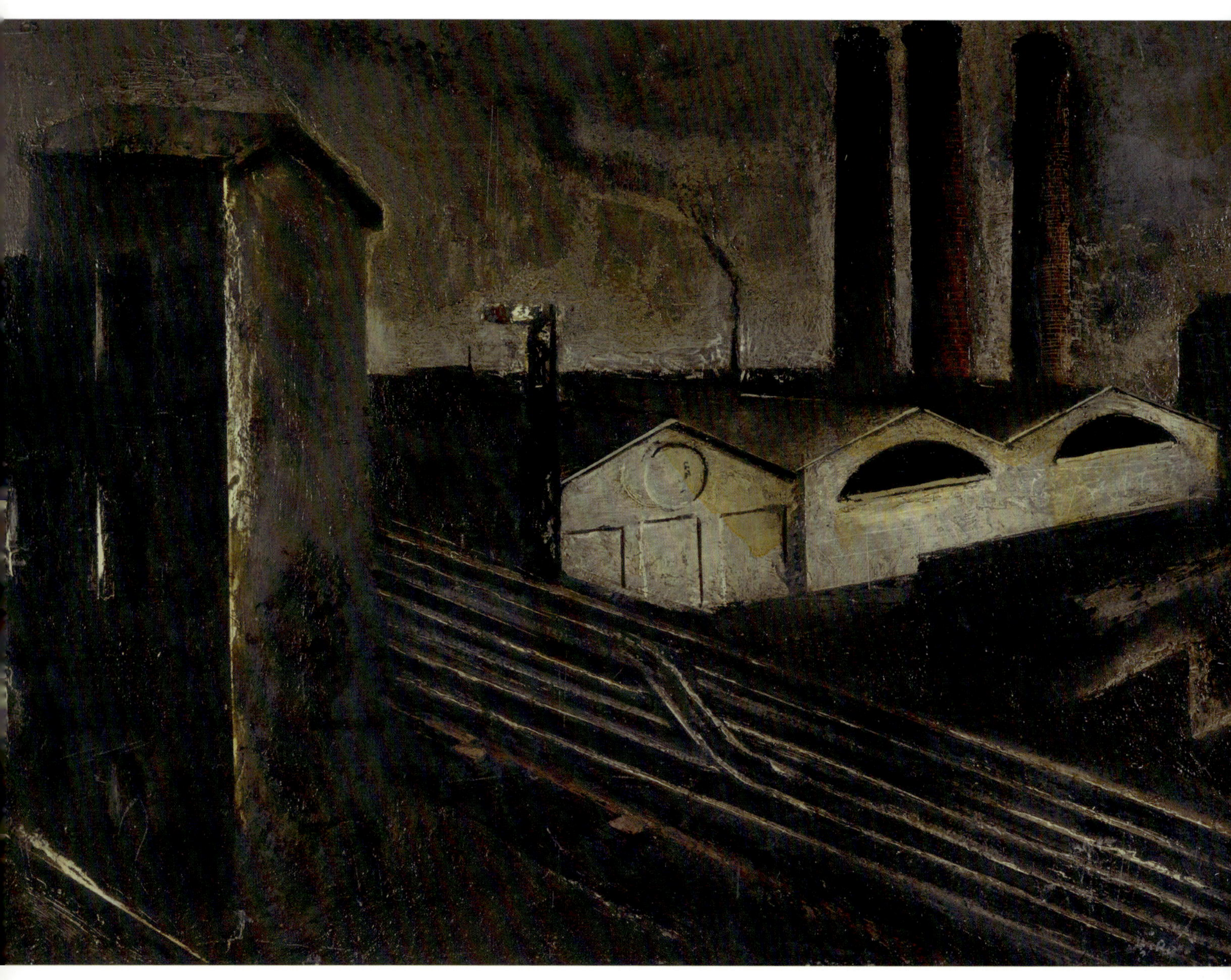

Mario Sironi
Urban Landscape with Chimney, 1930
Oil on canvas, 49 x 67 cm

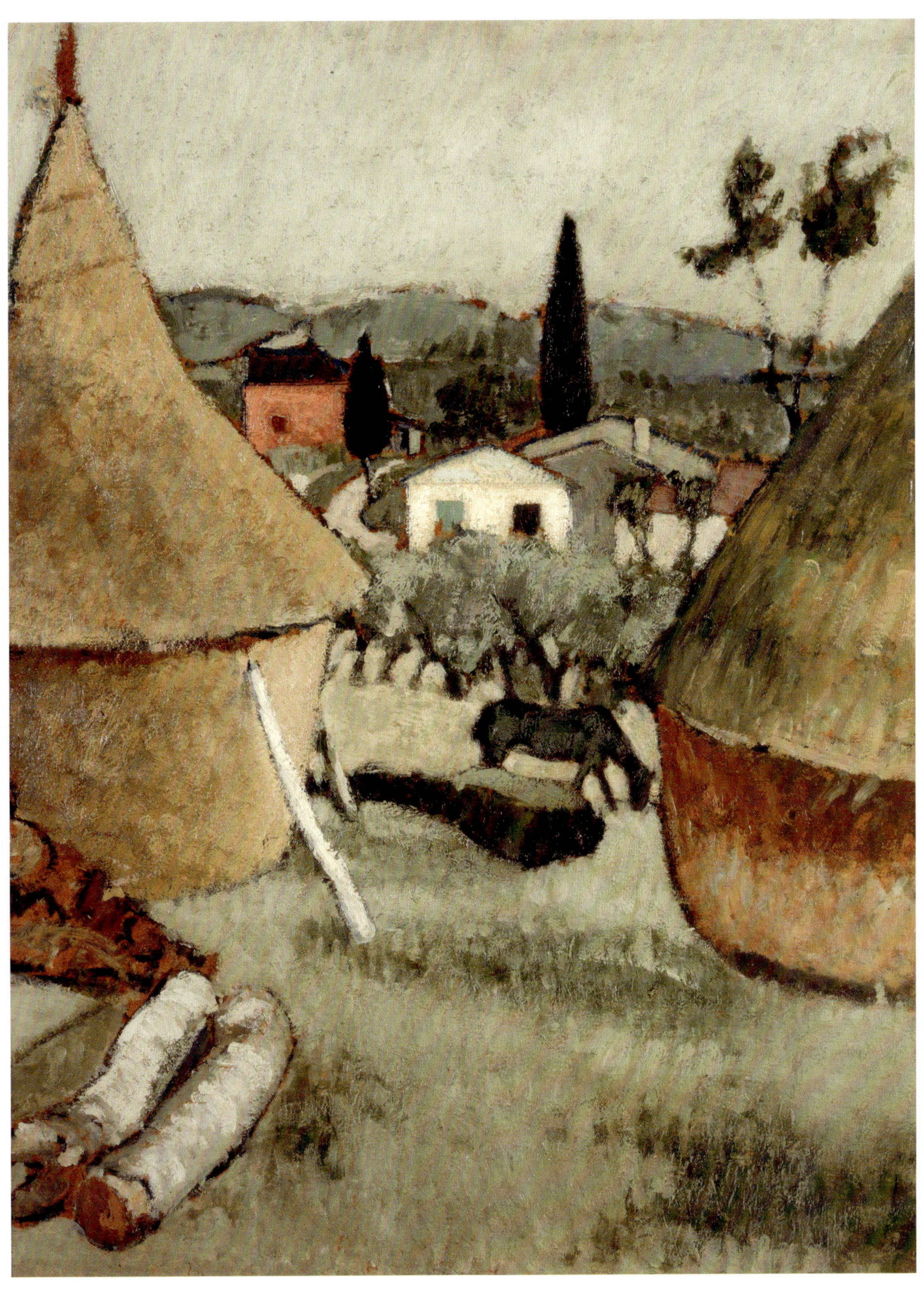

Ardengo Soffici
Santa Cristina, 1908
Oil on card, 64 x 49.5 cm

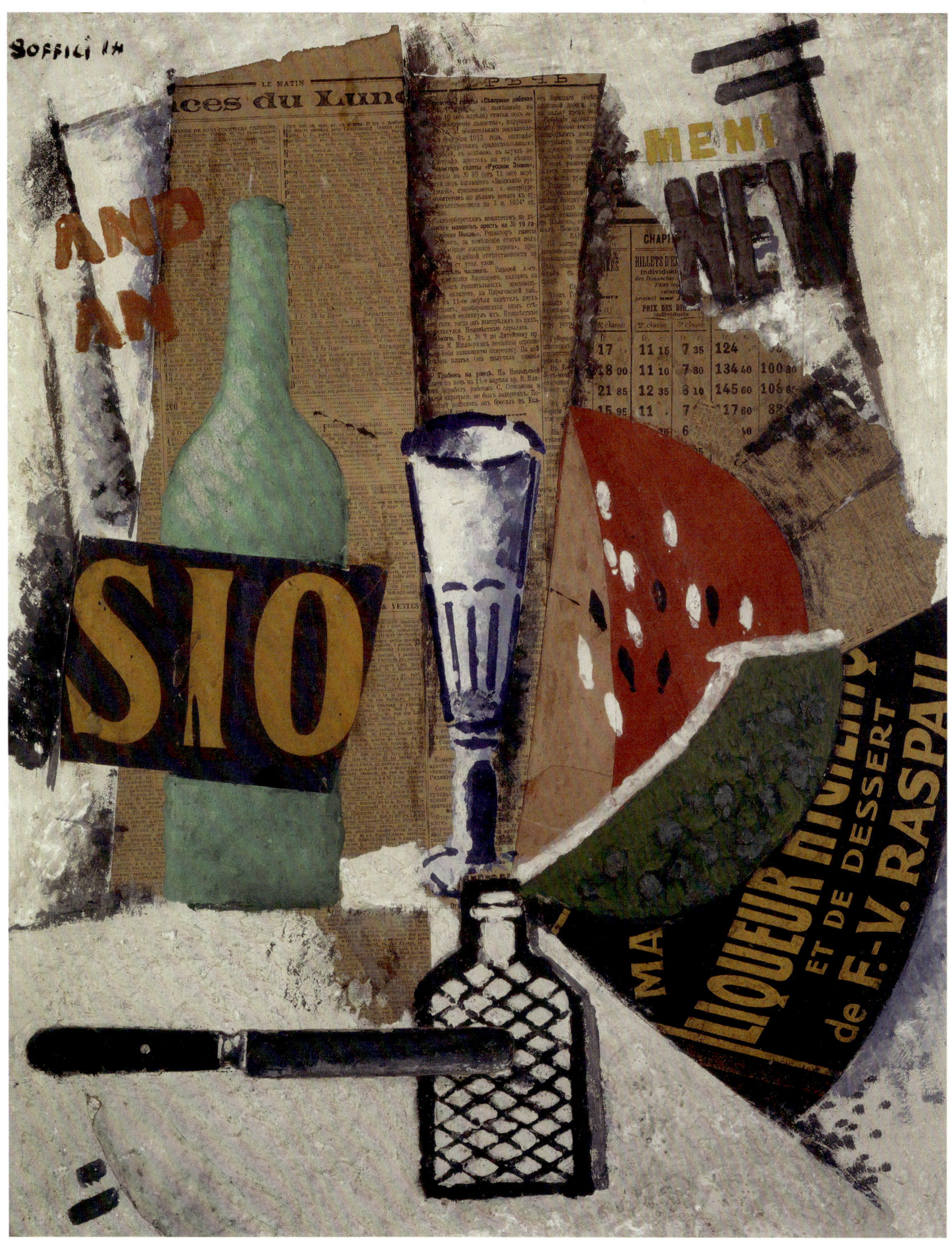

SOFFICI 14
LE MATIN
ces du Lunc
MENI
NEW
AND AN
SIO
LIQUEUR
et de DESSERT
de F.-V. RASPAIL
MA

Soffici began his artistic studies at the Academy of Fine Arts in Florence, but also demonstrated literary talents from an early age. Between 1900 and 1907 he was in Paris where he met and associated with the protagonists of the most important artistic tendencies of the day. He contributed to the magazine *Mercure de France* and, upon returning to Florence, founded the magazine *La Voce* with Giovanni Papini and Giuseppe Prezzolini. Although initially hostile toward Futurism, in 1913 he established a new journal with Papini named *Lacerba*, which eventually became the movement's official mouthpiece.

The Futurist influence is clear in *Watermelon and Liqueurs*, with its collage elements and sense of dynamic vibrancy – characteristics that were also typical of the work of another Florentine Futurist, Ottone Rosai. Nevertheless, Soffici's alignment with the movement was fleeting, and his work of this time can perhaps more accurately be characterised as 'Cubo-Futurist': a style epitomised by his elegant painting *Deconstruction of the Planes of a Lamp* (1912-13, Estorick Collection).

Ardengo Soffici
Watermelon and Liqueurs, 1914
Mixed media and collage on card,
64.6 x 54 cm

Published by
Estorick Foundation
39a Canonbury Square
London N1 2AN

ISBN 978-0-9567868-8-3

www.estorickcollection.com